POSTGRADUATE STUDIES IN MOTHERHOOD

HELEN TREPELKOV

Black Rose Writing | Texas

ISBN: 978-1-68433-084-3
PUBLISHED BY BLACK ROSE WRITING
www.blackrosewriting.com

Printed in the United States of America
Suggested Retail Price (SRP) $18.95

Postgraduate Studies in Motherhood is printed in Chaparral Pro

To my parents, with love and gratitude.

POSTGRADUATE STUDIES IN MOTHERHOOD

We make a living by what we get, but we make a life by what we give.

Winston Churchill

Prologue

I love life, and I am very greedy for everything life has to offer. I am also extremely curious and like being in the thick of things. This is why I subscribe to more magazines than I can read, and why I absolutely refuse to throw them away before I have a chance to at least peruse them. When I don't have time to read an article, I just tear it out and it goes on the "to read" pile. Needless to say, this pile can become pretty huge and quite an eyesore, hence the constant debates with my husband as to the need for timely disposal of these unsightly papers.

So it was not quite by accident that I came across an article in *The Wall Street Journal* dated January 8, 2011, titled, "Why Chinese Mothers are Superior," about Amy Chua's book, *Battle Hymn of the Tiger Mother*, almost a year after its publication.

The timing could not have been more perfect. It was a seasonably chilly and nasty November evening, and my mood was very much in tune with the weather. I had become too cozily settled in my ways, too cooped up in my everyday routine. I was beginning to feel restless—with restlessness that neither a good book nor a great concert or such would cure. I was in desperate need of a challenge and excitement in my life, which I had been missing for some time. I needed something with staying power, something that would make me impatient to wake up in the morning. Those of you who have read Nelson DeMille's, *The Gold Coast,* and feel that I sound very much like John Sutter, no need to worry. The similarity is only superficial. I am pretty sure that I am under the radar of any Mafiosi, and besides, my longings were of a slightly different nature. They would be better summarized by the words of the famous Russian poet, Anna Akhmatova: "Body cannot live without sun / And the soul, without songs."

The article aroused my curiosity and my fighting spirit. I agreed with some ideas and I rejected others. I felt a great urge to share my thoughts on the subject of raising and educating children in the United States of America from the point of view of a mother with a different cultural background.

After a few days I was opening the Amazon package containing my copy of *Battle Hymn*. I was so eager to compare notes, I started reading immediately.

Ms. Chua raised issues I could certainly relate to. I have two daughters who were born and raised in the United States. I have a foreign background. My husband, Alex, always very busy at work, gave me carte blanche in all matters relating to the upbringing and education of our girls. This is about it, however, as far as similarities are concerned. Alex and I are Russian. At the time our daughters were born, the United States was totally unfamiliar territory to me. I was raised differently from Ms. Chua, and I did not, for better or worse, possess a strategy for raising children tested on many previous generations. If there ever was a Russian way of raising children, I was not familiar with it. Also, since the day my older daughter was born and to the very day my younger one had sent out her last college application, I was a stay-at-home mom.

It was certainly not the career path I originally had in mind.

I was the valedictorian in high school, graduating *summa cum laude* from arguably the most prestigious higher education school in Russia, the Moscow State Institute for International Relations, MGIMO for short, fluent in French and English besides my native Russian. I started postgraduate studies at a no less prestigious research institute affiliated with the Russian Academy of Sciences, Institute for World Economy and International Relations, or IMEMO. When I came to the United States at the age of 23, following my husband on his first overseas assignment, I received an offer to work at the United Nations. It was a non-professional position, but it was the best I could hope for as a Soviet wife. Instead, I chose to stay at home and raise our daughters.

I realized I was embarking on a potentially lonely and difficult journey. Many of my friends were shocked, however (politely) not commenting. Alex was supportive, but he just did not understand my decision. I could sense that my father, too tactful to explicitly say anything, was not very ecstatic with my choice either. My mother warned me not to expect to be treated like a hero, and not to feel like one either, but to do it only if it came from my heart. It did, and I followed its calling.

Our daughters are grown now. They are independent young adults and they both live and work in Manhattan. Reading the book by Ms. Chua made me look back on my life and reevaluate my own child-rearing experiences from the vantage point of a, hopefully, mature middle-aged woman. It was a lot of fun and very revealing in a lot of ways. In a matter of hours I was brought back in time with math homework, music lessons, science fairs, Halloween costumes, and volleyball games. I love our daughters and I loved raising them. I am very grateful to Ms. Chua for making me relive those years.

Eager to follow the timeless wisdom of the white queen's advice and begin at the beginning, I started to unravel my life. One fact after another, delving deeper and deeper into the years gone by, I looked for the one initial event, my very own first cause that propelled my life in the direction it took. It felt as if I was aiming a huge searchlight at my past, its beam highlighting only the most prominent events, the ones that had an impact, that somehow mattered, leaving the rest in the dark.

When our children were growing up, I always tried to know what I wanted to achieve and have a strategy. Tactics, however, were another matter. I did not always analyze my methods, usually just following my gut feeling. Often, I just felt I was right, but did not exactly know why. So I just kept doing my thing, looking for a rational explanation along the way.

I was galloping through life at full throttle, always short of time, always cramming into my days much more than I could handle. Now, I am amazed to see that what may have seemed at first blush a chaotic succession of random decisions and events was, in fact, an immensely logical affair where very little was left to chance.

Here is my story.

Chapter One

I was married at the age of 22, shortly after graduation, which was actually considered rather late. Quite a few of my female fellow students were already mothers by that time. One of my high school friends already had a five-year-old son, but she was an exception. Not surprisingly, my husband Alex graduated from the same college and majored in international economic relations, as I did. A few months later, exactly on my twenty-third birthday, after celebrating with our family and friends at the airport with a bottle of champagne, Alex and I boarded a plane to New York. He has been quite successfully married to the United Nations Organization ever since, and I have been quite successfully married to him. Sometimes, however, I am not so sure that he is aware of the latter.

Alex Trepelkov, my husband, is a great guy, but to fully enjoy his virtues, I have to take him with a grain of salt. This is a man married to his job, par excellence. Any more committed to it and he could be accused of bigamy. When I was six or seven years old, my father liked to tell our houseguests a joke, which I enjoyed very much and found very funny:

A happily married couple is celebrating their fiftieth wedding anniversary. The guests are impressed by the stability of their union and ask the lady how they made it work for so many years. "It was actually very easy," the lady replied. "My husband dealt with big important issues, like whether there is life on Mars, and I always took care of the little things, like our children, our house..."

Little did I know it was my future life I was laughing at!

It was a fun flight. The travel time being more than ten hours, it was a very long one, too. We were, however, neither tired nor bored. We were young, happy, and carefree. We quickly made friends with some of our flight companions and continued the merry birthday celebration, drinking more champagne and smoking. Smoking was still allowed in airplanes back then in the early 80s. As the time difference between New York and Moscow is eight hours, my momentous birthday was prolonged accordingly, as if to celebrate the fact that my nonchalant life was about to end.

When the pilot announced that we had started our descent into JFK, I looked out the window. The American soil lay below. Something stirred inside me. Without fully realizing it, I must have experienced something akin to the Jerusalem syndrome. I had probably felt somewhere deep in my subconscious that I was looking at the land that would become my home for many years to come. My face must have shown my emotions, as is always the case, because Alex asked me what the matter was. Poker had never been my game.

Soon upon our arrival, I was offered a job at the United Nations library. Soviet wives could not seek professional positions and this was one of the best possible jobs I could consider. I knew it would be hard, if not impossible, for me to pursue a career during our overseas trips, but it was one of the most interesting and well-paid jobs available. It was an honor and I knew it. I accepted the offer.

We were just beginning our married life and it was practically the first time we had to plan our finances. It was actually the first time we ever *had* our own finances, since we both had lived with our parents before the marriage and for a few brief months after, as was the custom in the Soviet Union in those years. I wanted to come up with a budgeting strategy. I felt the need to set goals for our whole life ahead. I was excited and enthusiastic, tantalized by all the new prospects of making a home for us.

My future lay in front of me, very appealing, but also very unclear, like the early morning fog. The world is so perfidiously cruel in its noncommittal neutrality. Life is what you make it. I was observing, listening, taking in the busy buzz around me, the eager anticipation of the newly arrived, and the satisfied superiority tinged with a shade of jealousy of the departing ones...

The shortage of consumer goods in the Soviet Union was notorious. People tried to stock up on clothes, electronics, and kitchen appliances. My own stance was still very vague, but on an emotional, rather than rational level, it was starting to take shape. My internal homing device was firmly set on happiness. I needed a mechanism to secure it. I reasoned that since there was no limit to our possessive cravings, no limit to amassment of wealth, money could never really bring happiness, for one can never have enough of it. Keeping up with the Joneses felt like a disquieting and futile approach. I did not want to fall into the trap of mere consumerism, chasing the forever-eluding ghostly mirages of materialistic paradise and becoming a voluntary slave of my own greed for the rest of my life. I needed a finite goal.

This is when I had a brief moment of revelation, a breeze of a thought that only love has this quality of finality about it. I looked at love in general and at family life in particular, in that new light. Materialistic desires mean an endless search, which resumes every time you exhaust your desire of the moment. Love, on the other hand, is bottomless, never-ending, and inexhaustible. The finality of love is precisely in the infinity of the feeling. True love gives the rare state of absolute satiety, of blissful stillness. You don't want anything else, you have it all.

Don't get me wrong. I love the good life and luxury, and I enjoy tremendously every opportunity I get to experience it. I even start to drag my feet if I stay in a five-star hotel, unwilling to leave its premises. This means a great deal, in my case, because I'm usually the one out with the sun, sightseeing and exploring new places for hours on end. The first things I look up before going to a new place are the sunrise and sunset hours, to know exactly how much time I have to explore. But I can just as easily accept a more humble abode if the circumstances require it. I just never had any particular lust for money; it was never a huge factor or moving power in my life. Simply put, I was never truly in love with money, and I did not want to settle.

I feel that entering adult life—coming-of-age—could be compared to attending a buffet dinner. It is a litmus test of our upbringing, of our previous experiences, of our perception of life. If we come too hungry, we tend to pig out indiscriminately, eating too much and too fast. Coming ignorant, we tend to miss the opportunity to try new and exotic food that would be beyond our means otherwise. On the other hand, coming too greedy makes us half-choke on exquisite treats we cannot appreciate or enjoy. Jonathan Swift is credited with saying, "Brave must have been the man who ate the first oyster." I am pretty positive buffets make many people brave enough to consume ad nauseam exotic delicacies they have neither the affinity nor the appetite for. The results vary, ranging from mild discomfort to severe indigestion. One would be hard-pressed to blame them, however. As most of us mere mortals have monetary constrains, it does make sense to take advantage and try things we would not be able to try otherwise. But I feel it is a very slippery slope. We lose our freedom, little by little. We forget what we like, and fall prey to our greed, grabbing the most expensive items. Isn't it the same with career choices sometimes?

I came to my smorgasbord of adulthood with a rather cavalier attitude. I was not hungry, but curious and eager. I was excited by all the smells, sights, and sounds of the magnificent experience we call life. I was looking for something unique, something ethereal, of heavenly beauty.

New York was a coveted destination. We could not wish for a better start. I was happy, but not ecstatic. I did not consider it a particular blessing. I looked at it as a natural course of events; I did not know any other life. In other words, I took it more or less for granted.

Chapter Two

I was born into the family of a Soviet diplomat. All of my childhood years were a patchwork of my father's various long-term overseas assignments on which we joined him, and of his much more frequent shorter business trips when we stayed home, my mother, my brother and I, in Moscow, waiting for his return. I still remember the sad longing feeling at hearing an airplane pass over my head when I was just three or four years old.

In June of 1968, my father had an assignment at the United Nations European headquarters in Geneva, Switzerland, specifically, the International Labour Organization (ILO), a specialized agency of the United Nations. I was ten years old and had just finished the third grade. Preparations were swift, we did not have a lot of luggage, and soon a night train was carrying us west, toward a foreign country, toward a different life. I was clutching my biggest doll Olga, named after my maternal grandmother. I never really played with dolls, but my parents suggested I take it, realizing how miserable I was to leave my grandmother behind. I loved her very much, always.

The next day, we had to change trains in Vienna. In the evening, before boarding the train to Geneva, we went to a restaurant for dinner. Russian speech was not often heard in Western Europe in the late 1960s. People stared. I was on my best behavior, sitting with my back straight, making sure I cut each time but a small piece of my steak (steak would become the entree of choice during my childhood) and used my knife and fork properly. My hard work produced the sought-after results: an old and rather mean-looking waitress commented on my good manners, as I overheard my parents discussing later at night. I was gratified. I felt like it was my duty to stand by my father, to help him do his job. I felt relevant. I thought all the eyes were staring at me, judging me, sizing me up. I had to be up to par. This feeling would remain with me for a long time.

Eating out was not exactly part of our lives. Restaurants in Moscow were mostly quite formal, and parents were rarely accompanied by their children. In general, one usually went to a restaurant in large groups, to celebrate some especially important event, like a professional degree or an anniversary. The only time we went to a restaurant in Moscow, all four of us, was to celebrate my father earning his PhD. He wrote it during the nighttime, the only testimony to his sleepless nights the mounds of pine nut shells on his desk in the morning. Pine nuts, often still in cones, were abundant in the Soviet Union at that time, and he consumed them in huge quantities to give him energy and keep him from falling asleep.

I remember that day. Prior to our dinner, my father went to have a haircut and a shave at a barbershop. He took me along. I remember him so well on that day, young, happy, and solemn, smelling of an unfamiliar aftershave. We picked up my mother and brother and went to one of the restaurants not far from our house. I do not remember the meal, but the dessert was decorated by two small merengue mushrooms.

My only other encounter with professionally cooked food and places to consume it was during the summer previous to our departure for Geneva, when we spent my father's vacation, a whole month, in Lithuania. We drove there, and it took us three days to cover about 650 miles. No wonder. Of course, we made frequent stops, but I also remember the empty two-lane road and my father proudly announcing our speed being fifty miles per hour. We had no tape recorder of any kind to help us endure the long journey, but we did not need any. My brother, four at the time, would recount by heart the children's books that had been recently read (and reread) to him, and he did it with so much feeling and gusto, we all laughed nonstop.

We dined in restaurants on the road and went out practically every day while there. It was usually for a late lunch, considering my brother's age, and I enjoyed these outings a lot. Not so much for the food, however, as for our stops in the forest on the way back. My brother would take a nap, and my mother would quickly pick wild strawberries, later supplanted as the summer progressed by blueberries. After my brother woke up, we all ate them for dessert with condensed milk.

Early the next morning we were approaching Geneva. My father, who had already been there for his job interview, was very excited and anxious to show us this beautiful city. "Wait," he said, "there, after the next bend, you will see the Geneva fountain." His excitement got hold of me, too, and I was impatiently waiting to see something amazing. And there it was, indeed, a majestic and glorious sight.

Soviet children abroad were required to attend the Soviet school, which at the time had six grades. Younger kids, like my brother, were allowed to attend local schools, as long as they attended the Russian classes organized for them on weekends, as well as on Thursdays, which was a free day in the Swiss school. I was already too old for this scheme.

On September 1, the official first day of classes in Russia, my new backpack full to the brim with new notebooks in bright and shiny covers and pens and pencils in every imaginable color, in the highest of spirits, I went to school.

All subjects but French presented no difficulties, and I joined my new class smoothly. French was another matter altogether. What a nightmare it was! My grade had been studying French for two years already, and living in a French-speaking environment certainly sped up the process. I remember the agony of memorizing a poem around Christmastime. I was studying French for four months already, but it still was six or eight lines of almost nonsensical syllables. It would probably have been easier for me to memorize part of the DNA sequence at that point. But that was the first time I did it. I remember my teacher nodding her head in satisfied approval of my achievement. I got my first excellent grade in French that day. I think I still remember the poem:

Le vent d' automne passe, / emportant à la fois / les oiseaux dans l' espace, / les feuilles dans les bois...

It took me more than a semester to catch up. It would have been longer if it weren't for my mother. She did not speak French and was taking lessons herself. She translated every word of every text and of every assignment beforehand while I was in school, to make things easier for me. She spent hours every day doing so. Then we would spend hours doing my French homework.

One of the major turning points in my life came when I had finished the sixth grade of the Russian school and was supposed to go back to Russia and continue my education there. My parents did not like this idea. They decided I should stay with them in Geneva, attend the local Swiss school, and do the Russian school curriculum on my own, with occasional help from the teachers. I fought against their decision all summer to no avail. I wanted to go to Moscow and study with my Russian peers. I stayed in Geneva, as did a few other kids from my class. I was 13 years old.

The Swiss primary school had six grades. It was followed by the secondary level of three years, the so-called *cycle d'orientation*, or the orientation cycle, which completed the compulsory education.

In 1971, when I entered the *Cycle d'orientation de Budé*, there were four options, based on the test results upon the graduation from the primary school: Latin, Scientific, General and Pratique, or Vocational, the highest of them being Latin.

My parents wanted me to go to the eighth grade, in accordance with my age, and to the General section, not to overburden me with too many subjects outside the Russian school curriculum. The idea was for me to just study French by immersion. The primary focus was still on my Russian school curriculum. To study Latin seemed to them an extravagant idea altogether. The study of German was compulsory, yet other Russian kids who attended Swiss schools were usually excused at their parents' request.

I took a series of obligatory tests. The math part seemed easy, since the Russian curriculum was more advanced. The French part was more complicated. I remember the whole thing vaguely, but I do think I had to find patterns in strings of French words, synonyms, and antonyms. I was supposed to underline the words I did not understand. They were many.

Shortly after I took the test, my father got a call from the school administration. I believe it was the director himself calling. He told my father that he would definitely recommend the Latin group for me, but he also suggested considering my going to the seventh grade since that was the last grade when French grammar, orthography, verbs, and vocabulary were studied as separate subjects. My father didn't like the idea of me attending one year below my age, and Latin did not seem at all necessary to him either, but I was around, and I did like the suggested plan. I did want to study French in-depth as French-speaking children were supposed to do. The tests made me realize how poor my knowledge of French still was.

The idea of going to the highest group and studying Latin was also very exciting, and I did not want to give up the opportunity of studying German either. So in September of 1971, I wound up studying three foreign languages—French, German, and Latin. It was then that I came up with an uncomplicated but efficient method of studying foreign languages that has worked for me ever since. I would read as much as I could in that language and learn ten new words a day. After a while I would not be able to find ten new words, and I would bring it down to five. Sometime later, I would bring it down to two.

Once, our class had a meeting with the director of the school. After talking for a while about our current scholastic issues, he asked all of a sudden why we chose to study Latin. Then he pointed at me specifically and repeated his question. "I just love it," I replied. He said it was the best possible answer. I was doing what I loved, but it was not enough for me at that point. I wanted to excel at it. I am convinced that if we truly love what we do, we are bound to succeed. I do not believe in unhappy love. True love is always mutual. The trick is, in my opinion, not to confuse love with ambition or infatuation.

I finished the seventh grade on top of my class and was offered to skip a grade in the middle of the next year and go on to the ninth grade. I did. I had to give up Latin at that point, but I was able to catch up with my German during the winter break. Call it vanity if you must, but I did enjoy the look of consternation on my German teacher's face when he handed me back my quiz with a six (the highest grade in Swiss school) on it the first week after I skipped a grade. At that time I also started learning English as an extracurricular activity. I finished the ninth grade on top of my class as well.

Two months before my father died, he told me about a conversation he had with one of his younger colleagues. It was during my father's second assignment to the United Nations European headquarters. More than ten years had passed since I stayed there with my parents and went to the local school. By that time, I was already married and living in New York. I presumed this man's child was attending the school I went to. The man asked my father, as a person who had lived in Geneva for a long time and over the span of many years, whether he knew that Russian girl who went to the College de Budé many years ago and was still remembered by the teachers as a very gifted student. And my father replied, "Yes, of course I do. It is my daughter."

He did not say anything else, and I did not ask any questions. We understood each other without words. I am happy I gave him this fleeting moment of parental pride and glory. And I am glad he told me about it.

How much I wish, however, I could have given him more than just promises of potential success. Only now, thinking back, do I understand the depth of his despair at seeing me throw away my chances at a successful career. He was a very tough man, but he had always allowed me to make my own decisions, and never pushed his way with me. He kept his thoughts to himself. Those who wanted to hear them, listened. It makes me sad to think how much I must have disappointed him.

Interestingly enough, I had essentially similar episodes in both of my schools. The first one occurred after my first Russian spelling test, in my fourth grade. The semester had barely begun when my parents were summoned to the school. I was accused of copying the work of my neighbor, who was an excellent student. I don't know what my parents told the teacher, but they all but ignored it with me. They were secure without being arrogant. They just treated it for what it truly was—a misunderstanding. I rarely made spelling mistakes, and it was quite natural on their part. Still, I was happy and grateful that they chose to trust me. I valued trust, such a precious commodity in general, and their trust in particular. I did not have to gain it since it was the starting point of our relationship. I was presumed worthy of their respect and trust, and I was very careful not to lose it.

The following day I had to change seats and join a less outstanding student. All the hoopla notwithstanding, there was never a question of punishment. My next test still had no mistakes. The incident was forgotten.

The first few months in my Swiss school were hard, due to my insufficient knowledge of French. I did not always understand what the teacher was saying and what was expected from us. During my first math test, I was rather harshly reprimanded by my math teacher for copying my neighbor's work. I tried as best as I could to explain to him that I was just looking over to try to figure out what the assignment was. Rules were very strict as far as copying was concerned. It was penalized by a zero grade on the spot. No explanations or laments usually worked. The teacher had an imperceptible moment of hesitation and did not take my paper away after all, but I doubt he really believed me, judging by the look of slight uneasiness when he was handing the graded papers down during our next lesson. I don't remember exactly what grade my neighbor and by then my new friend got, but my work could not have been copied from hers. It had no mistakes.

In the Swiss school, failing to bring in textbooks, special quiz notebooks, or any of the essential school items was also penalized. We were given a grade for "discipline" every two weeks and a half-a-point was taken off for every such occurrence. It was called an *oubli*.

Grades were usually administered in half-grade increments. Every question or task on the quizzes was worth a certain amount of points. The grade was given strictly in accordance with the amount of points one received. It was thus very objective. The personalities of the teachers and of the children had practically no influence on the grade. Except, of course, my first math teacher. As I write this, his name comes to me from the depths of my memory and more than forty-five years that have passed. I hope I got it right. I know I got it right. Thank you for trusting me, Monsieur Chevalier!

The Swiss kids were not crushed in the least and took their zeroes very philosophically. Apparently, they learned early on to abide by clear-cut rules that could not be contested or broken and to pay for their mistakes in accordance with their age and the nature of the offense.

My one and only attempt at cheating during my school career proved to be a great disaster. The accounting exam in my third year of college was considered one of the toughest exams required for my major. And it certainly was, mostly because it involved a great deal of memorization. I decided to make my first ever cheat sheet. I spent quite some time putting all the material in minuscule handwriting on small sheets of paper. When it was done, I just pinned the papers to the lining of my skirt and went to take my exam. When I came to the examination room I realized that I had lost the product of my labor on my way to school. I was not devastated by it. I knew all the material. Nevertheless, I took it as a sign that cheating really was not my cup of tea. Maybe a less philosophical explanation was in order and a quick and efficient remedy would have been to just pin the stack of those sheets to my skirt when I was in school already. Somehow this simple thought did not cross my mind back then, which was for the best. Making the cheat sheet was more of a way to try something new. The main point of studying for me was to get to the bottom of things; it was a desire I could not resist. I had to know. Difficulties only made studying more exciting.

My most shameful cheating-related episode, however, was one where I didn't even think about cheating. I was taking exams for my secondary education degree certificate. It was a chemistry exam. I was at the blackboard, and I wrote the answers to the first two questions. The third one was so easy I didn't bother to put it in writing on the blackboard. All of a sudden my physics teacher, who was part of the examining committee stood up, passed by me, and slipped a piece of paper in my pocket. I did not realize right away what it was. It turned out to be the answer to the question. I was never more ashamed in my life. I did not know how to react. I just put the paper in my pocket. I was very good at physics, I liked and understood it much better than chemistry, and this lady liked me and apparently thought I deserved a gold medal, whether I knew the answer to that chemistry question or not. She was one of my favorite teachers. Yet I was never able to come up to her and explain that I knew the answer to that question and deserved my excellent grade.

In the evenings, I had to keep up with the much more complicated curriculum of the Russian school. I got all the help I needed or wanted from my parents, but I was not told what to do or how to tackle my task, and I was not monitored closely. I was the older child, deemed sensible enough and for the most part left to my own devices, which suited me just fine. I valued this freedom tremendously, since I have always liked to roam free, to work at my own pace and be my own boss.

I also needed hands-on experience. One of my father's favorite expressions comes to mind—"Stupid people learn through their mistakes, smart ones through the mistakes of others." The reason he had to say it so often was my constant urge to test every maxim myself and not to take anybody's word for it. The smartness behind his and my mother's approach was not to force me to listen, but to let me try and find out for myself that they were right, as a rule.

I remember one episode especially well, since it was a rather brutal one. I was learning to ski. I spent hours on the bunny slope and was feeling restless and ready to move forward. At last, one fine day, I decided I was ready for a more challenging slope. I got too carried away and considerably overestimated my skills. I chose a very advanced blue slope. Skiers were coming down so beautifully and effortlessly, I was sure it would be a breeze of a descent. By the time I managed to get down, my knuckles were bleeding (it was a warm day, and I had taken off my gloves against my own best judgment), one of my skis finished way before I did, and overall, my descent was not a very graceful sight. I think it was one of the best life lessons I had ever learned.

My parents did expect a lot from me always, nonetheless. Once, when I was already in my late forties, I complained to my father about the hardships I had to endure during one of my car trips to Washington, DC, because I had gotten a flat tire. I was telling him how I had to pull over in the middle of nowhere, how I called Triple A, and how a policeman had to help me put on the donut. At this moment my father interrupted me, and unperturbed in the least by my complaints, asked me with great surprise bordering on disapproval, "Helen, how come you don't know how to change a tire?" My father was a very good driver, with more than sixty-five years at the wheel. The last time he drove was the day before he died at age 81. During one of my last visits he asked me, "Aren't you scared to drive alone all the way to DC?" I felt sad. It had never occurred to him to ask me this before. I realized he was getting old.

I did my own planning for my studies. I was creating weekly calendars with self-assigned material to cover. The most ill-fated subject was chemistry, assigned to Sundays. That was the subject I had the most trouble keeping in check since we were always going to the mountains on Sundays, to ski or skate during the wintertime, or to have a picnic and play cards, board games, or *pétanque* in the summertime. Or we would just drive to other towns and cities, close and far, with our portable *Uher* recorder playing some Russian and French songs in the evenings to prevent my father from falling asleep at the wheel. My father made mixed tapes himself—it was the time of reel-to-reel recorders, even cassettes were not yet known—from the LPs he bought locally or in Moscow.

Many times, when we had stayed for too long in one place or another and had a couple hundred kilometers to cover to reach our next destination,

inquisitive faces were lurking everywhere. My father cautiously told them he would satisfy their curiosity when we had finished the meal. The Cold War was in full swing, and sometimes our being Russian was not taken very positively.

It had been a particularly hot day, and my mother wanted me to cover my head—a very sensible thing to do. The problem was, however, that she wanted me to wear a wide-brimmed straw hat. I was wearing shorts that day, and my personal sense of style absolutely revolted against this combination. I refused to wear it. No wonder that by lunchtime I was exhausted from the sun, and it made my bowl look especially big, and the spoon especially small. I wanted to get it over with. Ignoring the spoon altogether, I drank directly from the dessert bowl.

My parents froze. They were in shock that I could do such a thing. Our family had very strict table manners. We were supposed to eat properly always, alone or in company. So much so, the personage of Jennifer Lopez in the movie, *Party Planner,* made me smile in recognition. There was a tacit understanding that as far as manners went, we had to be on par with royalty. My father did not tell the waiters we were from the Soviet Union, after all, but said we were from another country of the Eastern Bloc instead.

Speaking of royalty, during one of those travels I saw the most beautiful young man I had ever seen in my life. Maybe the surrounding atmosphere of surreal beauty had reinforced the effect and contributed to the fact that I still remember this experience. I cannot tell now. We were in one of the Istanbul museums, admiring the displays of dazzling precious stones and jewelry. I wandered away from the rest of the family, enjoying the cool twilight of the halls after the scorching Turkish summer sun. I lifted my eyes and saw a slender young man, walking slowly from display to display. Somehow the words "young man" are not quite appropriate. I thought I was seeing a young king, so regal and dignified was his walk, so graciously was he carrying himself. He was wearing what looked to me, not very savvy in the sartorial intricacies, an impeccable suit. A man carrying his jacket followed him, or so it seemed. I was absolutely unfamiliar with the concept of servants, and all my undivided attention went to the young man, so I can't be sure of this now. I guess that was one of the rare occurrences of my praying, because this was exactly what I was doing, asking God to make the man approach me. He did and asked me if I spoke English. I would have never used the adjective "swift" to describe my father, who was beginning to gain some weight by that point, but he darted to the man before I could open my mouth and said, "She doesn't speak English." And that was the end of it. I still remember the exquisite profile and a very short-lived, but nonetheless very intense and unmistakable sensation of falling in love and a very new and powerful feeling—the power of being a woman.

The first time I prayed was when we went to see one of the most famous peaks in Switzerland—the Jungfrau. We spent a wonderful day wandering about and taking in the beautiful scenery. Getting closer to the top of the mountain, however, required a special train trip, and consequently cost extra money. I don't think I remember any price of any product from those years, but I do remember this one. It was probably 1970 or 1971. Each ticket cost forty Swiss francs. It was not a negligible amount for us, and my parents did not foresee the expense. The blessed time of credit cards when you could spend more than you carried with you, let alone more than you earned, was still many years away, so my parents were anxiously counting their remaining francs.

We have never been a religious family. The predominant religion in Russia is Orthodox Christianity. This is the branch of Christianity Russia adopted from Greece more than a thousand years ago and the religion of all of our faithful relatives, which were not many. The only one of my family members who was openly religious was my great-grandmother, Ekaterina. She was the only one who had icons in her house, in huge elaborate silver frames. This is why I was always a little uneasy when I had to stay alone in her living room. I always felt I was being watched. I had never seen her pray, yet the process going on in my head on that trip was nothing short of a natural prayer, so passionate and profound was my desire for my parents to have enough money to board that train. It is not that I expected to see something especially beautiful. I was too young at the time to read ahead and have goals or expectations for our trips. Quitting halfway, however, was not good enough then. I had to go all the way to the top, pun not intended, to see all that had to be seen, to do all that had to be done.

By the age of 15, when we drove from Geneva back to Moscow upon completion of my father's assignment, I had seen an enormous amount of the priceless treasures and breathtaking sights of Western Europe. One of the few European countries we did not visit was Spain. My father had dreamed of seeing Madrid and the Prado Museum for many years (I had been shown the Prado album for the first time when I was six or seven), but Russia had no diplomatic relations with Spain while General Francisco Franco was in power, so we could not visit the city. My father got to see his beloved Prado when he was already in his fifties. Interestingly enough, so did I.

After a week-long car trip from Geneva through the southern Italian part of Switzerland and almost all of Italy as a farewell tour, passing through the former Yugoslavia and Hungary, we crossed the border of the Soviet Union. At the border, my father went inside the Customs building to take care of the formalities. We were bringing a car of a foreign make into the country. My mother, my brother, and I stayed in the car. Immediately, we were surrounded by a huge crowd. Foreign cars were not a frequent sight in Russia in the mid-1970s, even in one of the major entry points to the Soviet Union on its western border. My mother did all the talking, so I was not exactly paying attention. I think it was just a mild interrogation session on the part of one man in particular.

"Where are you coming from, where are you heading?" he asked. We all remembered the finale, however. When he saw my father coming back, the man concluded approvingly to my mother, "You speak our language very well." She was too shocked to answer. He was already a few yards away, lighting a cigarette and talking to his friends about something totally unrelated.

United Nations employees in Geneva were granted diplomatic status starting at a much lower level than in the US, which was incidentally the subject of constant bouts of jealousy from their New York-based counterparts. So we had the CD acronym, standing for Corps Diplomatique—Diplomatic Corps—on our plates, which should have, theoretically, tipped people off. These letters, however, in all likelihood, did not say much to the majority of the crowd and remained just another enigmatic and unfamiliar inscription.

And so we continued our trip home. In those times there were not many tourists on the Russian roads, and some intersections did not have clear road signs. At times, we felt like mythic heroes from the Russian folktales, standing at a fork in the road, huge expanses with no cities nor villages in sight, trying to figure out which way to go. After one such bifurcation, we were still moving slowly, as my father tried to figure out whether he made the right turn. All of a sudden, a militiaman, as policemen were called then, jumped out of the blue to bar the road, his hands wide apart. Even my father, who was not easily taken by surprise, jumped in his seat. He had barely time to break. It turned out we were on a service road to some military object, and foreign citizens were not allowed to take it. As our car had Swiss plates, he obviously assumed we were foreigners. I remember his huge smile of relief when he learned we were not. The prospect of bringing us back to the main road at gunpoint was clearly not very appealing to him.

Within a month of arriving home, I entered the ninth grade of a specialized school with French as the foreign language, arguably one of the best in the city. I got back just in time. Without studying in Russia for the last two years, I could not get my maturity certificate and apply for college, since the quarterly reports from those two years were required to get the certificate.

Two years later, at 17, I graduated from high school with a gold medal, which was awarded to those who got excellent grades for the last four semesters and on the final examinations, passed the admittance exams, and entered the Moscow State Institute for International Relations.

I was taught well and learned a lot, but I did not experience any challenges akin to those of my early years. Studying came easy. The field of economics provided enough food for thought and research, but it was not appealing enough to get my undivided attention. I was going through the motions, but nothing really moved me. I was not sure what I wanted to do. I was on the lookout. I knew the intoxicating feeling of loving what one does, and I did not want to settle for anything less.

***

I had worked hard all those years. And yet, I was still *terra incognita* as a person. It was not because I did not have to break a sweat, but because I was working out of a well-appointed ivory tower. You do not learn yourself by narcissistically looking in the mirror. You find your boundaries through interactions with other people. There was a buffer between me and reality. I was basking in the amniotic fluid of family love and support, easy success, and recognition. I was protected against the shocks and the sharp corners of the real world. It was hard to let go of such bliss. I was not in a hurry. I was a cocoon—a cocoon that had yet to tear open.

Shortly after I started college, my father got his second assignment to Geneva, and I went there for two months during the summer vacations to visit my parents. I took summer French courses at the University of Geneva. After a quick exam, I was placed in the highest grade group, and I really enjoyed the delightful subtleties of the French language we were learning during those classes.

After classes, I would head straight to the language laboratory and try to cram some more French into the two or three hours I could stay there. It was not that the laboratory closed early, but there was a force stronger than my desire to listen to every available tape, and that eventually would get the best of me and make me leave, reluctantly. That force was *hunger*. The courses ended around lunchtime, and every day I would go to the university cafeteria first. Every single day, I would carefully examine the row of sandwiches that would make my mouth water, and every day I would decide against purchasing one, after all. They seemed to be outrageously expensive to me. I was absolutely sure that my parents would not refuse to give me the money, and I actually had it on me every day, but I felt it was an unjustifiable expense and would end up just buying a small cup of coffee.

Practically every year, we would take a cruise from Venice to Yalta, a port in Crimea. We would then take a train to Moscow and I would go back to my studies come the new school year. I had no particular difficulty getting good grades and graduated from college five years later, *summa cum laude*. I enrolled in IMEMO for post-graduate studies. Then I got married.

I was also still comfortably snuggled in my cocoon. It was a time bomb. The cocoon was bound to hit the hard surface of reality and burst, sooner or later. The source of my greatest happiness in childhood and in adolescence was bound to be the cause of my biggest challenges in life. It was the cause, but also the weapon, to deal with them.

Chapter Four

I was about to start my new job at the UN library when I learned I was pregnant. My husband was told by his bosses that it did not make sense for me to start working for just a few months, then taking maternity leave, most likely never to return. Indeed, it would have been extremely difficult for me to have a child and continue working for the UN. The only option we could have considered for a babysitter would be to find another Soviet wife willing to take care of the baby for a small remuneration. But we were living in Manhattan, where very few Russian families lived at the time, which made it practically impossible to find such a person. I had to pass the position on to another Russian woman.

My maternal instincts did not kick in until I was already pregnant. Alex and I did want a baby, but at the time it was more of a romantic notion for me. I did not fully realize what having a child entailed. My interests were someplace else altogether, in the familiar realm of academia. When these instincts did kick in, however, it was with the full force of a young healthy body. More than twenty years later, when I once recalled that time for some reason, I was shocked to realize that I had a choice. I could have had an abortion and continued with my life as it was. I would have started working, and my life would have probably taken quite a different course. But I was so mesmerized and so enchanted by the idea of having a child that the thought of choosing work over having a baby had never entered my mind. What was amazing was that I knew perfectly well that other women did have abortions in similar situations, but it had never occurred to me to have one myself.

During the first few months of my pregnancy I had rather severe morning sickness, exacerbated by the scorching heat of a typical New York summer. After the dignified slow-paced refinement of Europe, the skyscraping city of concrete, steel, and glass with its colossal energy and frantic beat fueled by human dreams and human sweat alienated me rather than appealed to me. I could not keep up with it. I felt intimidated by the hordes of people marching up and down its avenues, shocked by the sight of yuppies, scattered like numerous dark specks all over the white marble steps of the imposing downtown buildings, hastily eating their lunches out of disposable containers, or the male ones with their ties swung over their shoulders gobbling up their food on the go. Even the stores, after the small and cozy European boutiques, seemed beyond my grasp, and in my mind looked more like huge hangars.

I felt as if I were in a giant toaster. Many times I had to hide with my, by then indispensable, paper bag in the shadow of yet another tree in an incongruous-looking concrete planter. But nothing could have ruined my feeling of unworldly happiness. Having a new life in me felt like the biggest mystery and the biggest wonder on earth. I wanted this baby, and I was expecting it every single day of my pregnancy.

A few days after I found out I was pregnant, I went outside to have a cigarette. I lit up and took the first puff. At that moment I had a vision of my baby, curling up helplessly, trying in vain to avoid the nefarious fumes. I extinguished the cigarette and never took one again for a very long time.

Later, when the girls were growing up, I tried to inculcate in them that women did not smoke. I had to confine it to *women* because Alex has always smoked. It would have been foolish to do it explicitly, I was aware that this was one of the decisions they would make much later themselves and which would ultimately depend upon many circumstances beyond my control. Still, I was trying to keep them away from ladies who smoked. It is not difficult with young children, and early impressions are sometimes responsible for the choices we make much later in life. It was worth a try and could not hurt. I did not even realize how admirably I succeeded, at least until Lydia, our older daughter, was six years old. The girls and I were strolling through a park when we passed a woman who was smoking on a bench. "Look, Mom," Lydia said, visibly astonished. "A woman is smoking!" The lady was not baffled in the least by my daughter's remark and just glanced at us indifferently.

My cocoon tore with a loud crackle, with nothing gracious or elegant about it, and without much fanfare either. I developed a blood infection after childbirth. The doctors did not find the correct antibiotic right away, and for the first few days my body was fighting basically on its own. My temperature would reach dangerous levels, and when the fever would finally subside, I would wind up in a puddle of cold sweat. Too shy and too impatient to call for a nurse, I would unhook my IV myself and go, hugging the wall of the hospital, to check on my baby, who would usually be sound asleep in her transparent bassinet, behind a glass wall. Thus reassured, I would continue my journey to the bathroom, freshen up to the best of my reduced abilities, and then finally call the nurse to change my sheets and gown.

After I saw our daughter for the first time, my thoughts went immediately to my mother. I suddenly felt like I understood her on some completely new level, as if from within. I felt our invisible bond tighten.

At last the right medication was found and the fever gave way to a more manageable 38 degrees Celsius, and I was discharged from the hospital, with my baby in one hand and a pack of antibiotics in the other.

I was dealt a really strong blow. I was barely on my feet, holding on by the skin of my teeth. When we came home from the hospital, I remember Alex saying my face was the color of the white walls of our apartment. It was good old white, not ivory or eggshell, or any other such fancy shade. Definitely not soft blush. Looking in the mirror, however, was the last thing on my mind. I was looking at another face, the face of our daughter, and I felt awe and bewilderment, and incredulity, and stronger than anything, a feeling of happiness and completeness. I knew that the next day I would be alone with her. I loved her so very much and there was nothing in the world I wanted more, yet I felt I had no strength to lift a finger.

Our little baby Lydia was cold and scared in this huge unfamiliar world thrust upon her as suddenly as this new life was thrust upon me. She did not want to let go of me and would start crying the minute I put her in her crib. Once in a while she would stop to catch her breath and to assess the effect of her efforts. Her dark, alert eyes, surrounded by pointy clusters of long black lashes glued together by tears, were defiantly scrutinizing me, unyielding, unapologetic. I didn't know whether to laugh or to cry myself. At times, I was just tempted to yell back, "Go get it yourself, whatever it is that you want!" I needed sleep so badly. But I didn't want those eyes to lose their fire and become dull with lost hope and disillusionment. I was pretty sure that in order to become a fighter one had to be presented with the opportunity to win, at least occasionally. I did not want her to lose faith in the world just because I was too tired and weak. And so I would stand up time and time again, pick her up, and keep her close to me, giving her all my strength and tenderness, and all my love. The moment I would pick her up, Lydia would fall soundly asleep. Gingerly, like an acrobat walking on a tightrope, I would inch toward the crib. Alas, the very second her back touched the sheet the screaming resumed. Lydia was a very strong, healthy baby with a strong, loud voice.

By six o'clock in the evening I was so exhausted I could literally do nothing else. One evening, having squished myself into an armchair after putting the finally sound-asleep baby in her crib, I turned on the TV. To understand all the despair of this seemingly quite natural and benign gesture, I have to tell you that that was probably the first time in my life that I pressed the "on" button. I have never liked TV, always felt it was too slow-paced for me. I always have the urge to do something else while watching it, like browse through catalogs, or fix something. I watch it only to bond with friends and family and when I have no strength to do anything else. That was precisely the case on that night. *Three's Company* was on. It must have been quite a sight. A half-dark apartment, the glowing TV, the sound level next to mute, not to wake up the baby, and a shapeless lump of an emaciated pale young woman in an armchair in front of it, laughing hysterically, insanely, with total abandon. I must have needed this comic relief pretty badly. For many years, this sitcom became an indispensable part of my life.

It is amazing how a person can fall through the cracks in a modern, civilized world, and become invisible. I was alone without help until seven or eight o'clock in the evening, when Alex came home. It was not how I expected things to happen. Life threw me quite a curve ball this time. After organized effectiveness, my life became a complete mess practically overnight._My world was upended, and I had a feeling of losing ground and falling into total chaos and weakness. The little princess moved from her royal penthouse quarters into the dark cellar with a huge array of pots and pans to clean. And cleaning was quite a challenge at the time.

Physically, my life was a nightmare. I can't recall the exact way I was feeling, my body forgot it, thank God, but I do remember the torture of the dirty kitchen floor. The kitchen floor of our standard Manhattan apartment was covered with white tiles and got dirty very fast. I was lying down practically all day long, and I could see a good chunk of it from my bed. Not once had I washed the floors in my parents' apartment, but my mother kept the house immaculately clean, and the pitiful sight of those neglected tiles right in front of my eyes was driving me insane. And yet I had no strength to do anything about it. It was probably no bigger than twenty square feet, but it took me several weeks to muster the strength to finally start washing it.

At the time Lydia was born, breastfeeding was promoted forcefully. I was on large doses of antibiotics and I did not want them to enter her bloodstream, lest she develop allergies or other health problems later on. I remembered a few stories I heard in my childhood about children developing allergies to painkillers administered to mothers during childbirth. I did not know the details, but I wanted to be on the safe side. I had to withstand a considerable amount of opposition from the medical personnel who were trying to assure me that the baby was not likely to revert to breastfeeding after the bottle, because sucking from the bottle is much easier, in general. I felt strongly about the matter and obstinately persevered, grounding my judgment on the premise that babies are no fools. To my huge relief, when I was finally off antibiotics and resumed breastfeeding, Lydia gave up the bottle without blinking an eye.

Formula created another problem, however. It meant I had to prepare it. All it entailed, more or less, was the need to sterilize bottles every other day, but how I dreaded those days... It took me a few hours just to accept the inevitability of the task at hand. The job was almost unsurmountable for me because of my condition, and required so much effort on my part I had to sit down a few times to rest while doing it.

Yet despite my physical misery, I was happy with the newly found serenity and peace of mind. Never before did my life have bigger meaning and better and bigger purpose. Cynics would say that the maternal instinct is just one of the strongest human instincts, and sadly, they are probably right, but luckily we are allowed to bring the human touch to any of our endeavors.

Child-raising looked like a giant blank canvas to work on, presenting huge creative opportunities, but practically no guidelines. The enormity of the task at hand scared and attracted me at the same time. I was very excited to know this tiny new human being, but I was also acutely aware that this baby needed me and was fully dependent on me. More than anything, I was afraid to let her down. Motherhood felt like a real-life ethics exam.

Everything happened so fast—getting married, coming to New York, becoming a mother. Everything came relatively easy to me, too. The only problems I knew were of a scholastic nature, and even those were pretty tame. When I was in college, even talks among my friends about sleepless nights with coffee and cigarettes before the test made me shudder. Not once did I have to study past ten p.m. I never had a task that required the concentration of all my resources. I never really had to exert myself, never came even close to my breaking point. I was still a potential, unbeknown even to myself. Lydia and I were in the same boat, in a way, for I was a newborn, too. Not only a newborn mother, but a newborn person.

***

When, as a young girl, I walked into my office in the mornings during my internships and realized I would have to stay there until dark, I felt trapped. On top of that, office politics annoyed me. I was constantly tormenting myself, deconstructing my actions, realizing my numerous shortcomings, and seeking ways to improve myself. I knew that, strictly speaking, I should work on my "public face," but I had only one face—mine. It was far from ideal, but I have always preferred to work on myself so as not to be ashamed to present myself to the world, rather than look for a good mask. It has always felt like a deplorable waste of time and resources. You often see the slogan nowadays, "You don't get what you deserve, you get what you bargain for." I have always sucked at bargaining, as well. As far as being a parent is concerned, however, you report directly to God, and you don't bargain with God.

One day, when Lydia was eighteen months old, I decided to stop torturing myself and accept (and even enjoy) who I was. The word "overnight" does not do justice to the brusqueness with which I came to this decision. I remember the exact moment and place that it happened. We were coming home with Lydia after our walk in the park close by and had already entered the overpass leading straight to our building. It was safe to let the impatient little girl loose from her stroller at that point. I was watching her run happily toward the entrance, in her tiny denim skirt with a red cherry appliqué and a red tank top, a striped blue and white bonnet protecting her head from the August New York sun. And for the first time in my life I felt absolutely secure in who I was. It did not mean that I stopped seeking perfection. Self-improvement and self-education remain very high on my list to this day, if only to better understand and enjoy the world that I love so much. It meant that I had reached, at last, in my own eyes, the level of personal worth that allowed me to feel a legitimate part of it.

I don't want to glorify my life. I was pretty lonely at times. I missed the fun of seeing more of a grown-up community. I was never sure whether I really had what it took. I remember testing myself, while pondering the issue. I would try to figure out how it would feel in twenty years, with some of my friends and fellow students achieving great results in their professional lives and occupying prominent and respected positions. I would cruelly tempt myself by picturing my former rivals and people I had some grudge against on the very top of the social ladder. I must admit, it felt quite unsettling and I did feel the sting of regret and sadness. Then my gaze would fall on the profile of the baby sleeping in her crib, and I would smile.

Throughout my early years, I had been accumulating experiences, knowledge, values. The moment I faced real adversity, I started tapping into what I had accumulated. First, it was just the superficial stuff, but the harder I got squeezed, the more the deeper layers of my essence became involved, and I let go of my most cherished possessions. So when I had my moment, and my cocoon tore, I spilled out all the love. Now it was my turn to pay back by paying forward and passing it on. Amid the ruins of the old life, the chaos of a dirty house, a crying baby, and a failing body, the contours of the new one were taking shape, slowly, one day at a time.

Lydia's birth was my awakening, my moment of truth. What was I worth, when push came to shove? I was alone for all practical purposes, and for the first few months, sick and weak. Alex worked very hard and had little time left to help me. My family was far away. I was an ideal case study. Come on, show us what you've got!

Early on, Alex said that he had neither the time nor the possibility to get very much involved in the child-raising process, and gave me carte blanche in the matter. Alex had always loved his job and wanted to succeed. It required a lot of commitment, time, and effort on his part. I understood and respected that. It was the essence of his personality. To deny it, to fight it, to ask too much from him on the family front and jeopardize his career would have meant destroying who he was. I knew if he tried to give his family more time, he would not be able to succeed at his job, and that would make him unhappy. And I wanted him to be happy. I was once again left to my own devices. I felt that Alex's attitude was exactly what I needed anyway. I was used to operating independently. In fact, it was the *only* way I could operate. So the division of labor was perfect.

I did not advertise the deplorable weakness of my body, and Alex, very young and strong, was easy to dupe. I have many faults, and one of them, I am often told, is pride bordering on arrogance. Which in reality, I like to think, is nothing more than unwillingness to accept defeat too readily and also to complain.

I remember a time when I was five years old, playing outside on a confined playground, without any supervision. Older girls were jumping from what seemed to be a high wall at the time, but in reality must have been some border of three or four feet high or so. The girls left, and of course I had to try to do the same thing. I climbed on the wall. Looking down was a whole lot scarier than looking at it from below. I couldn't go back, however. I found a neat compromise. I hung on my hands. It was already too late when I realized that I was hanging on top of the stairs. I was old enough to know that I could break my back if I let go, but my hands were becoming tired and I knew I could not hold on much longer. People were passing by. I begged in my mind for somebody to take me down, but nobody realized how high the wall was for me and how afraid I was. I could not ask for help myself, however, since that would have signified defeat.

Well, when I couldn't hold on any longer, I let go. I landed safely.

Nonetheless, Alex tried to help take care of the baby whenever he had a chance. The seriousness and conscientiousness of his approach almost scared me. When changing diapers, he would put on tons of lotion and baby powder and massage all this goo into Lydia's skin. He had always believed that more was better, but I was not so sure in that particular instance. The baby's skin was so fresh, so delicate, it felt a pity to smother it with so many products. I could not help thinking he was treating our baby like a Thanksgiving turkey, but I did not want to hurt his feelings by saying anything.

He favored the same straightforward approach to swaddling. At the hospital, we were advised to swaddle the baby for the first few weeks. He was the only one of us who could do it properly. In my case, a small hand started working its way out the minute I was through, and I admit I enjoyed it. By the time our second daughter was born, swaddling babies was no longer insisted upon, which tormented by feelings of anxiety and insecurity in my still not completely familiar field of child-raising, I took as small validation of my maternal instincts.

When I was already strong enough, Alex thought some shopping would do me good and offered to stay with Lydia. The suggestion took me by surprise. Somehow such an idea never entered my mind. Merrily, I left the house and headed for Macy's, which was about a thirty-minute walk from our house. As I proceeded, my mood became less and less cheery and my steps slower and slower. About midway, I turned back. I realized I did not need or want any alone time.

Alex undertook another attempt, which proved to be his final one, at giving me some independence when Lydia was about six months old. I took a trip to Boston, and Alex stayed home with our baby. It was a fun trip, and I liked Boston a lot. But it did not feel right. Something very important was amiss. In my mind, I did not exist as a separate unit anymore. I did want to see the world, but I was willing to wait until we could do it together, as a family.

***

It was not easy to get in touch with our families in Russia in the early eighties of the last century. International travel was prohibitively expensive for us. There was no Internet and no Skype, and we could not afford frequent international calls either. The easiest and cheapest way was to change a few dollars' worth of quarters and use a public phone for a two- or three-minute conversation. The most common way to communicate was to write letters. It took about two weeks to get a reply by official mail. One could always send letters through friends and coworkers who were going to Moscow on business or on vacation, but such opportunities were irregular. There was no possibility of hiring a babysitter either. So there I was, alone and absolutely clueless about raising a child.

Chapter Five

For the first few months after Lydia was born, it was just pure visceral survival. I was not in a position to think about any child-rearing techniques. I was also blissfully unaware of the fact that according to a well-known adage, I should have started educating our daughter the moment she was born.

I believe the adage goes something like this: Conscientious parents ask a wise man when they should start educating their five-year old son. The man replies that they are five years too late.

To make things even more complicated, Lydia was a very active child and demanded constant attention. This cute little tyrant was pretty much running my life. She started walking when she was eight months old, and I was running after her at home and on the playground and never had as much as five minutes to relax.

When more than twenty years later Alex had a business trip to Bangkok and I tagged along as I often did, Lydia decided to join us. Nathalie had college exams and could not go. Alex had meetings all day long, and Lydia and I decided to take a flight to Chiangmai in the meantime. We were running late for our plane. It has always been my task to do all the groundwork and to lead everybody to wherever we had to be, but this time I got held back, juggling the camera, the map, the guidebook, the sunglasses, and since my sight was not 20/20 anymore, the reading glasses as well. At that moment, Lydia darted forward. She had already made some inquiries and was motioning me to follow her. Astonished, I was running after my baby all over again. Only this time, it felt so good to just follow her lead.

When Lydia was nine months old, I made a desperate attempt to go back to my studies. At that time, I had not yet completely dismissed my scientific career. I needed publications for my postgraduate degree, and I decided it was time I tried to write an article. I put all of my books on the dining table and placed Lydia on the carpet in front of me, hoping she would play nicely with her toys for a couple of hours, assured that I was at her beck and call in the immediate proximity. It ended in disaster. Caught up in the process and unwilling to lose my train of thought, I wound up placing the contents of my closet at the mercy of this insatiable child. I was at the end of my resources, and having emptied the container with my nail polish bottles as a last resort, gave her the look of a cornered animal. Lydia just shrugged her shoulders, as if to say there was nothing she could do. She graciously helped me clean up the mess for the next hour nonetheless. I decided to postpone my scientific endeavors until some more propitious times.

At the end of that week, we had company. I came into Lydia's room to feed her and put her to bed. I was tired after cooking and cleaning all day, and was not in a rush to get back to our guests. Lydia was lying on our bed, and I was lying by her side, holding her little hand and smiling at her. All of a sudden, she smiled back at me with a slow Mona Lisa smile and uttered her first "Mama" in a very soft, but very articulate voice. When I rejoined the crowd in a few minutes, I was ready to party until dawn.

And so it went. I was making Lydia stronger and she was making me stronger. Simply by needing me, Lydia was pulling me through. My daughter and I shared a secret. Long before I began educating her, she had started making a person out of me. Definitely, love is not a force of this world. The more we give, the more we get. In our material world, if you give one apple to your friend, say, Susan, you will be one apple short, whichever way you look at it. Not so, apparently, in higher realms. This crucial rule of love defies all the laws of the physical universe as we know it and feels counterintuitive at best. Love must be the gift from gods, a ladder to allow us to get closer to heaven or maybe just a result of their oversight.

The trips to the beach were the final touch in my physical recovery. Lying on the warm sand and looking at the ocean, so near, so huge, feeling its cool and salty breath on my face, had a calming and invigorating effect. I was running the sand through my fingers and had a feeling that the eternal energy encapsulated in every one of its tiny specks was entering my body. I was getting the vital juices from the earth itself.

Snippets of random conversations were coming to my ears, enveloping me and lulling me into a heavenly half-sleep.

"We just saw a horseshoe crab..."

"You'll have to make a step forward, Jimmy..."
"Give me your hand, Paul..."
The voice of my grandmother Olga was ringing in my head. *"Go hug this giant oak, Helen..."*

***

When I was a child, I spent all my summers in the country with my mother and brother, and usually my maternal grandmother, as was the custom among capital dwellers, especially families with young children. Russian countryside fascinates by its sheer vastness. There is nothing tidy or manicured about its miles-long rye and wheat fields and endless forests. Calm and strength emanate from this land. I liked to join my grandmother when she would go to a better-stocked grocery store of a bigger neighboring village to buy us food. It usually involved walking a couple of miles each way to buy bread, milk, cheese, butter, and other basics. I enjoyed these walks through the woods a great deal. I was four years old when I started accompanying my grandmother on these trips. No one thought it unusual, and I felt perfectly grown up, on an important mission to provide sustenance for my family. No one in the village had a car.

Cars were not as ubiquitous in Russia then as they are now. In fact, my father bought our first car when we were in the country one such summer. There is a funny episode associated with it. The neighboring house was rented by two rather pretentious women, a mother and daughter. Almost every conversation with them involved some serious name-dropping and mention of their numerous postgraduate degrees. They were probably just miserable and missed the city life, not unlike Carrie Bradshaw from the well-known HBO *Sex and the City* series on her outing to Suffern, New York.

Their pale inseparable figures, topped by matching summer hats, looked very much out of place. Their outfits were more appropriate for the French Riviera than a remote Russian village, with linden tree leaves permanently glued to their noses to avoid sunburn (sunblock was yet to be discovered by my fellow Muscovites). They had a look of sheer terror on their faces after bumping unexpectedly into the warm proofs of the local herd's passage. Our landlady disliked them a great deal. I think she felt protective toward us, her renters, two women with young children who were cooking, washing dishes, or doing laundry all the time and usually had no time to participate in highbrow philosophical discussions or fancy parties.

Not that my mother and grandmother could ever be called sensible-shoe kind of women. Indeed, neither of them owned a pair of house slippers until way into their late sixties, and even now my mother would not consent to anything but suede wedges. My grandmother did all the housework in a spiffy housedress and heels, to the utmost delight of my mother, who thought her mom was the most beautiful woman in the world, especially when she put on some lipstick, which she did whenever she went out with my grandfather.

Anyway, one fine day my father came to visit us, not by bus as he used to do every Sunday, but in a brand new Volga. It was the best car available for purchase at the time, and his face gleamed more than the metallic moldings of the car itself. Our landlady, who seemed to have a homing device for anything even remotely sensational, and the appearance of a private car could be considered such an event in those days, materializing seemingly from nowhere, stood there for some time, her arms akimbo, with a look of gleeful triumph on her face. Then she said loudly, addressing apparently no one in particular, "And I have to ask you, folks, who needs those postgraduate degrees anyway?"

***

My grandmother Olga was very intense, and I think I got my particular love for nature from her, and it started on those trips to the local grocery stores. Nowhere do I feel as deeply alive as when surrounded by nature. This is when I feel a divine presence. God dwells in nature. You come and communicate with Him, one on one.

Very often, she would point out a particularly magnificent oak tree and urge me to go and hug it, to borrow some of its strength, or breathe deeply when we were in the forest. We would pick mushrooms for dinner, and my grandmother would explain to me where to look for them and how to differentiate the edible ones from the poisonous. We usually followed the road, but once in a while, when the load was especially heavy, we would take a shortcut straight through the woods. We would never get lost. My grandmother could unmistakably find her way by the sun. Those were the most exciting moments. It felt as though no man had ever trodden those grounds. And very likely, that was often true. This place was situated relatively far from Moscow and other big cities in the area, and its charm and beauty had not quite yet been discovered by tourists and summer vacationers.

The forests of the region were mostly old pine ones. They usually had no underbrush, and we would carefully make our way on a thick carpet of prickly pine needles of seasons past, which cushioned our steps and absorbed the noise. The air was absolutely still and seemed imbued with the mixture of warm sunshine and the smell of sap oozing from the tree trunks. They stood there straight and magnificent, almost equally spaced, with the crowns lost high in the sky, looking very much like the columns of some ancient cathedral. And that is precisely where I would have thought I was if I were old enough to think in these terms. We called it Magical Forest.

I love places of worship. I was forever captivated when I saw the Duomo of Milan for the first time at the age of ten. Cathedrals, churches, monasteries, temples, and mosques of Rome, Florence, Venice, Siena, Pisa, Genoa, London, Paris, St. Petersburg, Athens, Istanbul, and many others followed in quick succession. My father also told me at some point about the cathedral in Cologne, and it became almost an obsession of mine to see it. It took me more than thirty years before I got to fulfill my dream, but I was not disappointed. Seeking to celebrate God, humans have produced the most beautiful and powerful creations. All the knowledge and talent of the best architects and artists, striving to bring about the beauty worthy of the Almighty, are immortalized in these works, and they are sublime.

During our shorter strolls through the woods with the rest of the family, my grandmother would instruct me and my brother on how to cover the wound with clay whenever she would notice some tree damaged by tourists. Or she would stop us all in our tracks to enjoy the beautiful vista from the high bank of the river that our country house stood on. On a clear day you could see for many miles ahead, and when gazing toward the villages on the lower bank, I think she was trying to spot the house where she spent the happy years of her own childhood, when her mother was still alive.

All vegetables and berries were bought from small makeshift markets near train stations. Very often, there were local farmers who would go door-to-door selling their produce. We quickly became regulars and enjoyed first dibs. We were very desirable customers indeed, because we would often buy all they had to sell. That was especially true when berries were in season. First came wild strawberries, then raspberries and blueberries. Local women would go to the woods at dawn to pick berries and try to sell them by the glass to urban vacationers later in the day. These ladies would usually make a beeline straight to our house with their wares. Their baskets would hold ten to twenty such glasses. I still remember my excitement when my mother would buy all the contents of those seemingly enormous baskets. Few things can compare to the taste of milk fresh from a cow, warm and a little frothy, still holding an imperceptible aroma of the fragrant grasses, with berries straight from the woods; or a skillet of freshly-dug potatoes fried with mushrooms you picked yourself at the crack of dawn, heading to the forest just as the sun was waking up and starting to hug the still numb and sleepy earth with its pink, barely warm heavy rays. The silence of the morning forest would be so deep, so engulfing, so absolute, you felt compelled to stop in your tracks and listen.

I remember the smell of the bonfire in the evening or that of the pine tar when I popped the gooey ball of it between my fingers; the intense blue of a cornflower, glowing in the twilight in a rye field; delicate blue bells and cheerful daisies. The porcini mushrooms with a few pine needles still stuck to their delicate velvety caps. Whenever I think about those years, my memory conjures up images of absolute carefree happiness. Such were the glorious days of my early childhood, drenched in sunshine, pristine beauty, and love.

Chapter Six

When I was strong enough to enjoy looking at a cute baby in a stroller for the first time since Lydia was born, I learned I was pregnant again.

I read a few books on pregnancy, the ones my doctors suggested and let me borrow from their office, with vivid interest. Now, with the Internet, when information is just a click away and so readily available, new parents are very well versed in all the intricacies of the process, efficiently texting and tweeting, exchanging experiences and ideas, posting with delight evidence of their successes on Instagram and Facebook all the while. It looks like the millennials take literally the saying that one picture is worth a thousand words and prefer just to snap it and to be done with it.

Much more can be achieved much faster nowadays. When our kids were growing up, information was harder to come by. It did not chase you, you had to chase it. Where there is a will there is always a way, but I just was not interested enough. When Lydia was a baby, childcare seemed to be part of the realm of haute couture, while books tried to squeeze all the riches and wonders of such a complex and diverse subject into the Procrustean bed of pret-a-porter.

Besides, the only time I could consider getting things done was during Lydia's afternoon nap and a couple of hours in the evening, after I put her to bed at around eight and Alex and I were finished with dinner ourselves. As the day progressed, the to-do list became longer and longer. There was no way I could squeeze it all into the few short hours, and the debates in my head as to what to prioritize were becoming more and more feverish. Doing what seemed to be at the time a very inefficient process of fishing snippets of information from books on childcare never made the cut. If anything, I used any moment of free time I could to fill in the blanks of my knowledge of New York life in general, and in particular, homemaking in America.

My source of choice was *The New York Times*, with its Sunday Book Review and *The New York Times Magazine*, especially the William Safire column on language. I also liked the Friday Arts and Leisure section. My absolute favorite, however, was the Living section, which appeared every Wednesday. I would start waiting for it with vivid anticipation come Thursday. The vibrant quick-paced life of New York was bursting and spilling over the newspaper's pages. I was imbibing this potent mixture of information and good vibes and it was helping me to regroup, to regain control over my life.

The heavenly midday respite was very short-lived anyway. One day, when I was already pregnant with Nathalie, I was desperately trying to get Lydia to nap. She was only two and a half years old, after all. I had high expectations, as I was hoping to snag a half hour of sleep myself. Sleep was the one thing I lacked the most and was desperately craving all those years. If only I had a kingdom, I would have traded it for a few hours of sleep in a heartbeat.

I had been reading, telling stories, and singing to Lydia for some time already, and had completely exhausted my repertoire and my strength. I decided to just lie down with her and hug her and drifted off. I awoke with a startle. All the awful things that may have happened to the naughty child while I was asleep zipped in my head before I even opened my eyes. I found my daughter quietly sitting by my side and waiting patiently for me to wake up. Obviously, from that day on, I never tried to make Lydia take her nap.

Until Nathalie turned two, I had just one night of uninterrupted sleep, with the exception of my hospital stay after childbirth. Miraculously, both girls slept through that night, and I woke up feeling well rested for the first time in five years. My humble instant Folger's had never tasted so good, and I quickly donned my fancy morning gown. Life felt great. My morning coffee still gives me particular pleasure, the memory of that day forever ingrained in my brain.

I did manage to get acquainted with the staples of childcare, nevertheless. I got hold of a copy of the famous book, *Baby and Child Care*, by Doctor Benjamin Spock. Had I known more about the author, had I understood where he was coming from, I am sure I would have been much more receptive to his teachings, but I read his book out of context, and the then revolutionary character of his approach—to trust our instincts and not be afraid to show love to our children—was lost on me. It just seemed to me the obvious thing to do, I was not even aware that any other approach existed. The popular catchphrase of those years, "Have you hugged your child today?" sounded like a gentle reminder not to get wrapped up in the everyday annoyances, not like a novel or even controversial statement.

I recall looking at the table of contents and seeing titles like "Terrible Twos" and something like "Awful Threes," and the fours did not seem to be any better. It came to me as a big surprise. I remembered my younger brother at this tender age very well. He was a most enjoyable child. One of our favorite games was called "Give Me Your Hand" and consisted of climbing from one piece of furniture to the other without touching the floor. I used to give my brother my hand and drag him behind me from couch to credenza to armchair around the room. We had a lot of fun playing together.

When our girls hit that presumably difficult age, I was very apprehensive, in view of all the warnings. It turned out to be a false alarm. Neither of them threw any tantrums; the only thing that made my life unbearable at times was their inexhaustible energy. My own source was rather depleted by the evening despite the fact that I was quite a young mother by modern standards. I would have preferred to settle quietly with a book following our afternoon playground time instead of having to build castles out of the sofa cushions, and to make sure the girls didn't get hurt jumping on them, and trying not to lose my mind from the deafening warrior shouts that would usually accompany those activities.

Another problem I was totally unaware of until I read about its existence was the likely jealousy of the first child toward the newborn. My parents must have handled this issue well, for I could not relate to this at all. I was four and a half when my brother was born, and I associated myself more with my mother at that point than with the cute little baby brother of mine. I felt like a grown-up as far as he was concerned, and I was excited as much as everybody around me and eager to welcome the newcomer into our family. I must admit, however, that coming home from the hospital with my mother and my newborn brother Sergey was probably the most enchanting memory of my childhood. Flowers were everywhere. Every corner of every room contained a doll for me and gorgeous bouquets for my mother from my father and his coworkers. I don't remember any particular toy or any particular flowers, just the feelings of astonishment and bewitchment. It felt like a fairy tale.

My own idea of preparing Lydia for the arrival of a sister was very simple. It did include toys, but it was centered on the spiritual component. I referred to the new baby as *our baby*. The most memorable activity was letting Lydia listen to Nathalie's heartbeat. Lydia would run to me very willingly whenever I called her and quickly put her ear to my belly, but I wasn't aware of the fact that she probably did not entirely share my enthusiasm until a much later time.

When Nathalie was born, Lydia was two months short of turning three. She was very patient and understanding about the fact that I needed about one hour to change, feed, and play with Nathalie before she went back to sleep several times during the day. Lydia would play quietly, never once interrupting me. I did not realize the depth of her misery until she made a suggestion. "Why don't we put Nathalie in a suitcase and ask Daddy to take her to work with him?" She must have been mulling over the issue for quite some time before she came up with what must have seemed to be a perfect solution for her. Feeling that my methods had pitifully failed, I remembered one of the "dry" techniques and ran out to buy presents for Lydia to bribe her back into enjoying her sister. A method I did not believe in, for the record, the die-hard idealist that I was, but the incident scared me so much I was prepared to make a concession.

Nathalie, being the younger child, had an altogether different outlook on family ties at the same age. We were strolling in the woods once, when she was two and a half years old. We passed a huge colorful caterpillar, which could probably be called beautiful if you are into such things. A few yards down the road we saw another caterpillar, just like the previous one. All of a sudden, Nathalie rushed back, carefully took the first one, and placed it near its double, explaining her actions by saying, laconically, "Sisters." I would have never touched such an intimidating hirsute creature myself unless my life depended on it, so my major conclusion from that incident was that Nathalie would probably be a great doctor. She followed another gift of hers—a very precise and quick mind—and chose law school, but she was doing premed studies up until her last year of college when she decided to switch paths.

The fact remains, Nathalie was a perfect baby, if there ever was one. I am not sure I would have had it so easy if she weren't. For the first few weeks, she would wake up only to eat. She seemed to understand that I was there for her, and she saw no need to worry. Once, when she was seven months old, we all drove to Pathmark to buy groceries for the week, as we often did. The checkout line was unusually long, and I was thirty minutes late with the breastfeeding. I got frantic with fear, but Nathalie, warm and comfortable in a baby carrier on my belly, remained very serene. She just grabbed my finger tight and let go only when we came home and I started to feed her. My finger, however, remained numb for a few minutes.

I was more relaxed with my second pregnancy. By the time Nathalie was about to be born, I felt in control. I prepared everything. The house was clean and the fridge was well-stocked for Alex and Lydia to last the duration of my hospital stay. I even had a batch of handmade dumplings in the freezer. Nathalie was a few days overdue, so we kept eating those dumplings, which were actually pretty good, and I kept making new batches.

I didn't think of bringing a camera to the hospital when Lydia was born, so for Nathalie's birth I came prepared. Not only did I bring the camera, I also brought my best nightgown, to take pictures of myself with the baby. Very swiftly, happy to be back to what I thought was my normal self, figure-wise, I put my arms through the armholes. And, oh horror, I got stuck. It turned out I didn't shed the extra pounds as fast as I had after my first pregnancy. I was not in total control, after all. Well, it never hurts to be reminded of the need to be humble. My disappointment was very short-lived, though, as few things could have ruined my mood that day, certainly not a trifling matter such as a few extra pounds. I decided to deal with the issue in due course, and enjoy my carefree life while I could.

The hospital food was not exactly bad. It was boring and bland, but since all I had to do to get it was put a check mark against the dish on the menu sheet, it was thrilling enough for me. I did get carried away and was putting check marks against all the dishes on the menu. The nurse finally scornfully told me on my second day that I could have only one main course, not three. My gluttony was due not only to a hefty appetite, but to the fact that mealtime was one of the happiest for me. First, babies were brought in for feeding. I would breastfeed Nathalie, and then my food would come. Instead of putting my sound-asleep baby back in her bassinet, I would keep her next to me, and would enjoy a long divine meal that I did not have to cook. It was paradise. Even now, I still think of the maternity ward as the happiest place on earth.

For a long time, whenever I spoke of my stay in the hospital after Nathalie was born, I would refer to those days as the happiest days of my life, to Alex's utter dismay. He had never really grasped how badly shaken I was when Lydia was born, and was genuinely shocked and even hurt that I would feel that way.

Truth be told, I was not just happy, I was in heaven. For the first time in almost three years, I could do whatever I wanted. By that I mean, basically, that I could sleep as much as I wanted, and I sure did take advantage of that opportunity. Whenever I was not sleeping, I would take long showers, style my hair, and apply mascara without always having to worry what Lydia was up to.

For the three days we stayed in the hospital with Nathalie, I never heard her voice. She never cried. I realized that when I was getting dressed and about to leave the hospital. I heard a baby crying in the hall in such distress, I had to go and see. I saw my daughter, in a tiny onesie, checked out and left in the hallway. She never liked the cold. Since she was born in December, I had to bundle her up when going outside, which I started doing the day we came back from the hospital. When we returned from those outings, Nathalie would continue to sleep so soundly, I would feel bad waking her up just to undress her. I would leave her in her warm clothes, and she would happily sleep for a few hours, clearly very comfortable.

Despite her seemingly genial ways, it was apparent early on that Nathalie was not to be treated lightly. Lydia had a friend who lived on our floor and would come to play with her from time to time. I would place Nathalie in the playpen near the older girls and watch them play. Apparently, Nathalie wanted to see what was going on more clearly, instead of through the mesh of her playpen. She was only six months old, but she would stand up and hold herself up by hooking her chin on top of the playpen. Her legs would be giving way, and occasionally she would waver, but she held on and made sounds to solicit some attention. Once, absorbed in her game and showing unequivocally that she had no use for it herself,

Lydia threw Nathalie a toy, a plastic boat. In a few seconds the boat was sent back with a might I was astonished Nathalie was capable of. She made it very clear she did not appreciate a disparaging attitude.

One of the first acts upon my coming home from the hospital with Nathalie was jumping on my scale. The situation was not very encouraging. I hardly gained any weight after my first pregnancy, but this time I was more than twenty pounds overweight. I was breastfeeding, so any quick fixes and rash diets were out of the question. The answer came quite unexpectedly. I saw a beautiful skirt by Christian Dior during the "white sale." It was long and pleated, in a nice off-white color. It was a dream of a skirt. The price was affordable, but the skirt was in my pre-pregnancy size. I bought it, nonetheless. Every day after Alex left for work I would hang it in plain sight. Every time I would feel like snacking (I especially liked Thomas' English muffins with peanut butter), I would glance at the skirt and put the food back in the fridge. I had oatmeal for dinner for three months. It is very healthy and very good for you, no question, but by the end of the third month I could not look at the cheery Quaker's face without becoming slightly nauseous.

Still, there is nothing like a nice piece of clothing two or three sizes smaller than your normal size to make you lose weight. Incidentally, this was the time I got confirmation that eating slowly to lose weight really works. Many times I would have to interrupt my meal to attend to one of our daughters' urgent needs. I was usually feeling so hungry, it required all my willpower. After returning to my plate a few minutes later, however, I would hardly ever continue with my meal. My appetite was gone. It took me six months to lose the extra pounds I put on, but I did it...with the girls' help.

By that time I felt in sync with New York. I liked the energy and the beat of this big, busy, brilliant city, moving steadily forward like a huge harvesting machine, pitilessly separating the seeds from the chaffs. I was firmly steering my stroller with one hand and holding Lydia with the other, on through the human ocean, in step with millions of its dwellers. After years of hugging the safe, welcoming coastline, I was about to embark on the voyage of my life, my hand resolutely turning the wheel toward the open sea. It was about time. I started looking for the right way to raise our daughters. I could not leave this process to chance anymore.

The way I perceive it, I was brought up mostly by personal example with occasional guidance and suggestion, but hardly any consistent pressure. I feel that our family life and the overall family spirit have shaped my attitude toward life in general, and education in particular, much more successfully than any mentoring or lecturing could have done. People around me were not making careers, or raising children, or doing chores. They were just living. The atmosphere was not overbearing, but it was not at all relaxed. No *dolce far niente* in my family. Life felt rather like a strong torrent, and I was entrained by it, and I enjoyed it. We all bonded, we were all part of one process, all working toward the achievement of the same goal, doing one big chore, everybody just a different part of it.

When I thought about writing this book, I asked my mother whether her mother had any particular strategy for raising children. "What are you talking about, Helen? She just loved us," my mother replied.

My parents certainly loved me, too. But it was more than just love. Or maybe it was what love is all about. It never occurred to me to fight for acceptance. I was accepted no questions asked, unconditionally. I was treated as a human being in my own right, as an equal and welcomed member of the family community. I belonged. I was enjoyed. This spirit got me hooked for life and I was always looking for and trying to recreate this atmosphere in our family, too.

***

I have very early recollections of myself. Some sporadic episodes go back to when I was three or four years old. The most important and uniting element to all of them was a remarkable feeling of happiness, security, and well-being. Another very distinct feeling was one of pride in my family. I felt I was very lucky to have my mother and my father as parents. Interestingly enough, I do not remember thinking about them in superlative terms, like the smartest one, the most beautiful one. They were just special, in a class by themselves.

One of my earliest memories is that of my parents dancing to the sounds of a huge grey Grundig in our apartment. It was still the time of reel-to-reel tape recorders, and I watched the little colored ends, dangling from the special slots provided to secure the tape in place. They swirled, as the reels slowly rotated, and very pleasant sounds filled the room. I was literally basking in happiness. It seemed as though some kind of amazing bliss was enveloping me.

It was my birthday. I had just turned three. All my relatives knew that building blocks were my passion, so I had about a dozen new sets in front of me, full of all kinds of building blocks imaginable. There were small square ones that were wonderful for building round turrets. There were shiny green ones in the shape of real bricks. There were rough unpainted wooden ones that worked best to strengthen the inside of the construction. The crown jewel of the lot was a huge wooden box with a sliding top. This was my parents' present. The blocks were so shiny they seemed to be wet. They came in four colors—blue, red, yellow, and green. There were round ones, square ones, and rectangular ones. There were arches and cones. At last I had everything I needed to build the castle of my dreams. It was time for me to go to bed. I was exhausted from all the excitement of the day and I didn't even mind, for I knew tomorrow was going to be a wonderful day.

***

My relatives are my foundation, each and every one of them tucked snugly in their place, as the building blocks of the castles of my childhood. They are all in me, in different measure, according to nature's master design, wherever fancy took it. I stand on the bedrock of their dreams and their doubts, their faults and their strengths, their defeats and their victories. Gone are their tender eyes, loving hands, soothing voices, but their legacy remains. Just as with the building blocks on my third birthday, the most prominent and the most colorful ones are my parents.

Chapter Seven

My father planned to become an engineer, like practically all the men in his family. But the war altered his plans.

On June 22, 1941, Nazi Germany attacked the Soviet Union. My father was 16 at the time and had just finished the eighth grade. On the first evening of the war, he and some other boys from his class were sitting on the roof of their school. Like thousands of other Moscow civilians—women, old people, teenagers, even children—they were there to help extinguish the incendiary bombs in case of an air strike. They had to grasp them with huge tongs and try to throw them down to the school courtyard, where they were no longer dangerous.

The first air raid took place one month after the beginning of the war, on July 22, 1941. Shortly after, a bomb did fall on the roof of the school, and the boys managed to roll it down before it started a fire. The next day my grandfather, ignoring my father's protests, sent him and his younger sister into the air-raid shelter in a subway station near their house. That night a German high-explosive bomb fell near that very subway station. It hit a beam and detonated without damaging the roof of the subway tunnel where everybody was hiding. After this incident my grandfather had to agree that the shelter was not really much safer than their house, and my father was allowed to return to the roof of his school, rehabilitating himself in the eyes of his friends who thought he had gotten scared and deserted them.

There was another incident in my father's life when he did not want to look afraid in front of his friends. My grandfather worked for the Ministry of Heavy Machinery at the time, and was sent on a business trip to a metallurgical plant, a giant of the first Soviet five-year plans, which was being built on the outskirts of Sverdlovsk (to which its old name of Yekaterinburg, given to the city by Peter the Great, was restored in 1991), in the Ural mountains. The family lived near the plant, out of convenience.

In winter, my father and his friends used to go skating on the ice of a nearby river.

The middle of the river never froze due to a warm current coming from the local power plant. One day the boys decided to see who could come the closest to the edge of the ice. My father did not want to seem like a coward in front of the local boys, and he came pretty close to the treacherous edge. When, having satisfied his ambitions, he turned to go back, he saw tiny bubbles of water under the ice on his path. He should have trodden carefully on the dangerous patch, even better, crawled over it, but a ten-year-old boy did not think of that. My father jumped. The ice cracked, and the next thing he knew, he was in the water. All the boys ran away, except for his one best friend. As my father later found out, they ran to his mother shouting, "Your son drowned!"

In the meantime, my father tried to get out of the water. Whenever he leaned on the ice, the ice gave way and snapped under his arms, but still, he managed to remain afloat and slowly move toward the coast, until he felt the firm ground under his feet. He remembered this first brush with death, the first-time realization that his life could end suddenly and easily, while keeping guard on the roof of his school. He was ready to fight for his home, his school, his city, as the noise of the approaching German bombers was getting louder and louder.

***

More than seventy years have passed. One early winter morning, I went into Grand Central Station in New York on a very prosaic errand. I wanted to clean my boots, all but destroyed by the sleet and salt mash of the city streets. I strolled past a long line at a local coffee stand, relieved that it was not the line to the shoe-shiners, which was much more modest, and then all of a sudden I heard music. A quartet of young violinists, trying to make some money, was playing Vivaldi in one of the passages. The strong beautiful notes, amplified by the vaulted ceilings of the building, were enveloping everyone and everything, like fairy dust from some magic wand, and transforming the otherwise trivial everyday activities into a truly special experience. Unable to leave right away, I joined a small crowd of early morning commuters who were as mesmerized as I was. The music stopped, and the crowd exploded with roars and cheers of appreciation. For a few brief moments, these girls made a difference in the lives of dozens of people.

This incident made me think of the young boys on the roof of their school. They all must have been scared to die, but just as the cold sticky fear of death was slowly crawling down their bodies and paralyzing their movements, a rage was rising as well. A rage against the difficulty of their lot and the unfairness of life. With this rage came a clear understanding that their generation had to earn their right to live, that in order to live, they had to face and defeat death. There was no way back and no side doors. War, it seems, does not allow for any shades of gray. It's either stark white or pitch-black.

They fought, and they won. And hats off to them, now and forever.

My father went to war shortly before he turned 18, without finishing the tenth grade. His small group of volunteers, four schoolboys and a dozen young men from the district factories, were sent to a tank school. Four months later, they were on the front line. It was the spring of 1943. The most difficult months for the Soviet Army, with the heaviest losses and the deepest retreats, were already over. My father's tank brigade retreated for the last time during the war near the very well-fortified city of Vinnitsa, in Central Ukraine (one of Hitler's Eastern front military headquarters, under the code name of Werewolf, was in the vicinity). That was the first time they had to fight against the German Tigers and Panthers. They retreated about 10-12 km. After that they were moving only forward.

The tank brigade my father was fighting with was used to strengthen the troops on various fronts, from the Baltic Sea dunes to the south borders of Moldova, and was engaged in many memorable operations. After the death of his predecessor in the beginning of 1943, the new brigade commander started by taking the earlier mentioned Vinnitsa. He also freed his native village, which was near Vinnitsa, hugged his parents and pushed forward, chasing the retreating German troops. It was also during that time that he sent the tanks over the railroad tracks winning back another well-fortified city. The Germans did not expect the Russian offensive from that direction, for the railroad cut through marshes, and this approach to the town was practically not fortified for that reason. Another major event was the crossing of the Dnestr River by tanks moving over the bottom of the river, on a low gear. All the openings were sealed with clay to prevent water from getting inside of the machines. Again, they emerged in a totally unexpected location, not in the shallow waters of the regular crossing.

An interesting episode, associated with the Sandomir Platzdarm battles, very heavy ones, took place when my father was working in Geneva many years later. While attending one of the diplomatic dinners, he met a Hungarian diplomat who turned out to have been fighting there at the same time my father was. Hungary was a German ally, so these men were shooting at each other at that time. Yet many years later, citizens of friendly countries, they were seated at the same table.

My father's most painful memory, however, was not one of bloody combats when the cries of dying men burning alive in the hit tanks were overpowered by the roar of the engines of hundreds of those steel monsters. The tanks churned up the earth and human flesh with their broad merciless caterpillars. More painful was the chilling sight of the empty Majdanek concentration camp near Lublin, Poland, amid the peaceful silence and the light caressing breeze of a nice summer day. The Soviet troops had just liberated its prisoners. Piles of corpses and neatly packed bags with human hair were everywhere. This was when my father nearly joined his fellow soldiers and got drunk for the first time.

These men hardened by war, men who did not flinch in the toughest battles, needed to put each of their days behind, and needed to forget. The soldiers would ask the village headman, soltus, on which farm the Polish moonshine, bimber, was made that night and would go get it and drink to try and forget the seen atrocities, if even for a short while. Many of them had relatives killed on the occupied territories or taken to labor camps. They could not help wondering whether the hair of their loved ones was in those bags, too.

My father always had a well-stocked bar for visitors, but I never once saw him pour himself a drink. He seldom drank alcohol. He told me his older fellow soldiers protected him from taking to drink. He did not say more, and I did not ask. I wish I did.

When the brigade crossed the German border, the first small town they encountered on their way was brightly lit and absolutely empty. In the morning, my father met a German in a black uniform. He decided it was an SS officer. He put his pistol to the man's chest and asked him, "SS?" The German waved his hands in fright, *"Nein, nein, Ich bin ein Eisenbahner."* He turned out to be a railroad worker and the owner of the house my father was staying in. He had come out of his hiding place, overcoming his fear, to check on it.

My father studied German in school. At the time, German was the most common second language in Russia, about half of all the schoolchildren were studying it. After five years of learning it, my father thought he did not remember anything but one or two phrases from his study books, like *Anna und Marta fahren, fahren nach Anapa.* But when he came to Germany, German words started to pop out of his memory. Very soon he spoke German fairly decently, and understood the language even better. As a result, after the war he was offered a job in the Soviet Military administration, first in Berlin, and later in Leipzig and Potsdam. He returned to Moscow only after the process of transferring administrative responsibilities to the officials of the future German Democratic Republic had begun.

The war had finally ended for him, and with it came another turning point in his destiny. For the first time in many years, he had to think about what to eat, what to wear, and how to earn money. Up till then, the government took care of all those needs for him. Now he was on his own. His number one priority upon returning home after demobilization was to get his high school diploma.

My father applied to the school for working youth. These schools were created after the war to allow young people aged 14 to 25 who had interrupted their studies to go to war or to work to support their families to resume their secondary education. He ran into the school director in the hall. He was a very nice man, as it turned out later, a handicapped war veteran. But my father found him to be rather inhospitable during their first encounter. It was early March, so the school year was already well underway. The director was very skeptical that my father could catch up. It would have been difficult even for a regular student, let alone my father, who had not been on a school bench for many years. He refused to accept my father's application, and seemed to be a soulless bureaucrat at that. My father was, however, very determined not to lose another year. He did a lot of convincing, working his way up, from one authority to the next, to no effect. Finally, he managed to make an appointment with the head of the city educational Olympus, if not the minister of the secondary and higher education himself.

The man allowed my father to resume his studies, just asked him not to get too many bad grades. My father was so happy he got carried away and promised to become a straight-A student. The man smiled and said there was an English saying, "It's too good to be true." My father did not know this saying at the time, but he liked it and used it with great pleasure later on.

In a couple of days, he was already behind the school desk. The troubles were far from over, of course. He had to work very hard. He had always been a good student, but he forgot a lot of the material he was supposed to know from the previous years and upon which the curriculum was obviously based.

He got a lot of help from his teachers, however, especially from one of the math teachers in the school. His own math teacher did not approve of my father's "adventurism," as he called it. But not only did my father graduate, he did so with honors, receiving a silver medal, the only medal awarded in his graduating class.

At the time, there were two honorary degrees in high school—a gold medal, awarded to students with only excellent results for all their graduation exams and all major high-school subjects, as well as for behavior; and a silver medal, awarded to those with no more than three "slips"—three "good" grades only were allowed. Math was the only subject my father got a "good" grade for.

A five-point grading scale was kept by the Soviet education system from the tsarist times. It had four basic grades: 5 (excellent); 4 (good); 3 (satisfactory); and 2 (unsatisfactory). 1 (complete failure) was a very rare occurrence, and usually signified the supreme stage of the teacher's indignation more than actual scholastic achievement, or rather the lack of it, in this case. There were also half grades, used in routine daily work, but not for official quarterly grades. The work had to have no mistakes to deserve a 5, one or two not-too-grave mistakes to deserve a 4, and so on. The system was not absolutely rigid, however, it did leave some room for interpretation.

The following year my father became a student of MGIMO. I knew this story from a very young age and was very proud of my father.

***

I had very similar feelings as far as my mother was concerned. Soon upon the return from their foreign assignment to Stockholm (my maternal grandfather had worked in the foreign trade field practically all his life), in March of 1945, Olga sent my mother and her brother to the country, to her mother-in-law, Ekaterina, in order to take care of all the domestic issues after their long absence. Since there were only two months of the school year left, my grandparents decided to spare my mother the stress of starting a new school at that time and let her wait until September to resume her studies. My grandmother did not mind her staying behind and repeating the third grade, but my grandfather would not hear of it, and insisted my mother go to fourth grade, along with all the other children her age.

It was at her grandmother's that my mother learned about the capitulation of Germany and the end of the war on May 9, 1945. It was a warm sunny day. Suddenly, the wife of Ekaterina's younger brother appeared on the deserted village road. Holding her head scarf with one hand and gesticulating vividly with the other, she was running, shouting, "The war is over!" laughing and crying at the same time. Ekaterina's younger son perished when he was 22 at the beginning of the war, during the Battles of Rzhev, also referred to as the "Rzhev meat-grinder" or "slaughterhouse" due to horrific losses suffered by the Red Army. So did her younger brother.

The euphoria at the mere thought that the mayhem was over, the glory of the moment and the pride in their people, the memories of the hardships endured and the personal sorrow fused into one almost unbearable emotion, and the two women remained for a long time together, clasping each other's hands, speechless, not quite ready to face it on their own.

The evening of that day the victory was celebrated by a religious procession, and one week later the villagers celebrated their first postwar wedding. The efforts of the whole village to find a white dress for the bride proved unsuccessful. The closest they could come up with was a light blue one. My mother, very curious, sneaked out of the house to go see the ceremony. The church was full of people. A pair of strong hands lifted her and placed her on a windowsill so she could see better.

The ordeal was over, and although for many of the villagers, happiness was merely a remote memory at that time, people were determined to claim their lives again. That was not a slow and shy awakening, akin to a delicate snowdrop on the first dry patch of the spring earth. It was a riot, a force to reckon with, as the dormant waters under the thick ice, confined for a long time against their will and then suddenly set free by spring, murky and dark at times, sparkling in the bright sun at others. It seemed like all the hopes cut short, all the unfulfilled dreams of the villagers were vested in this young couple. After the ceremony, the powerful human flow gushed into the street, celebrating the triumph of love over destruction, of life over death.

***

On September 1, 1945, my mother in her brand new uniform with big white bows in her two tight braids (school rules required girls' hair be braided), started fourth grade in an all-girls school of her district. Boys and girls studied separately at that time, to the chagrin of both sexes. The girls' uniform consisted of a brown dress and an apron, black for everyday wear, and white for special occasions, and hair ribbons to match.

Usually Olga referred to her son and daughter as her golden sun-kissed children. My mother remembers only two occurrences of her mother being upset with her. Both of them have a lot to do with her school uniform. Once, when my mother was still a child, she came home from school when her mother, having just finished waxing the floors, was putting the freshly washed and ironed white linen covers on the sofa. My mother had some very exciting news to tell her mother. In her excitement, she tripped and fell on the slippery freshly treated floor, and not realizing that her brown uniform dress got brown wax on it, she sat smack in the middle of the sofa cover, continuing with her narrative. Olga's disappointment was considerable. Many hours of hard work went to waste, but she took it in stride. Such trifles were not very high up on her personal scale of disasters, after all. She just sighed and quickly put the ruined covers back in the basin to soak.

The other incident, definitely more heated, took place on September 1, when my mother started her last school year, the tenth grade. Although not quite a child anymore (kids started school at eight at that time, so she was already seventeen), my mother stayed outside with her classmates after school to play cops and robbers. She fell a few times. Her new uniform looked deplorable, the spiffy skirt all but reduced to shreds. Her face, obliviously happy, showed no remorse whatsoever. My mother looked a little bit like Jane, the faithful friend of Tarzan, from the movie they all liked so much, but Olga was not amused. For a few minutes, she chased her daughter around the room holding onto the rag she was washing the floor with.

I do not recall any incidents of my mother being angry at me. When my brother was not born yet and I was about three, I climbed into a cupboard full of china and managed to drop the entire cupboard on myself with pretty much all of its contents. I have only a vague recollection of the event, but I remember very clearly my mother's first reaction. She was terribly scared whether I got hurt or not. She was quite upset about the china, too, sometime later when she was collecting the debris, and I was sitting very quietly, feeling guilty and upset. She had bought this china piece by piece, whenever she could save enough money for it. But I don't remember any punishment or any reproach, that time or on any other similar occasion.

Whether that was good or bad child-rearing, strictly speaking, I don't know, but seeing my mother, whom I loved very much, genuinely upset and not angry at me, made me take responsibility for my actions. I was not afraid of being punished, but I did not want to cause pain to people I loved. Subconsciously at first, because I was so young, I felt I had a rare gift of true love and I was grateful and careful not to lose it. I felt I owned the world, and in a way, I did. My mother did not have to be authoritarian. I have always tried to act preemptively.

I feel punishment engages the animal part in humans, our instincts of self-protection and survival, and not our reasoning. It trains us, breaks us, rather than teaching us moral values. I feel that if conscience, as an inner mechanism of making one follow a set of certain moral values, can be taught, it can only be taught by human instruments, since this is one of the human characteristics, par excellence. Consequently, in general, I don't think punishment by parents is a method of choice to instill morals in children. It is a method of maintaining order among adults when education has failed.

After the war, schools operated in two shifts, with an extra evening shift for working youth. They were not unlike busy factories, with four or five classes of thirty-odd kids per grade in each shift. There were thirty girls in my mother's class. Fathers of more than half the pupils were killed during the war. Their mothers did not have the luxury of choice, they had to join the workforce to support their families. Alone until late into the evening (the workday lasted until seven at that time) and having to take care of themselves and often also their younger siblings, these girls grew up fast. Many years later, they told Olga how they were protecting my mother from the prosaic side of life, lest she lose the idealism and innocence of youth. It turned out my mother had protectors in other, very unexpected, quarters as well. Again, many years later, boys from their building told my uncle Lev that the leader of the local bad boys had a crush on my mother, and all of his minions were strictly prohibited of even thinking about annoying the family in any way.

One of my mother's best friends at that time survived the siege of Leningrad. Her mother and younger sister did not, so she was being raised by her grandmother. As tragic as her story was, the utmost tragedy was the fact that it did not stand out as unique or even unusual. Her story was not an exception, it was the norm, just taken to the extreme. The unusual, the exceptional, was the long lost paradise of normalcy. The quiet uneventful life, with a welcoming home, a living, loving father, and a smiling mother greeting you with a warm meal and a warm word, bordering at times on boring before the war, were perceived as heaven.

School started at eight o'clock in the morning to accommodate the three shifts. Every morning, my mother would be ready well in advance and go sit by the warm radiator and patiently wait until it was time to leave for school. Schools were not heated at night the first winter after the end of the war to preserve precious energy, and sometimes pupils would find ink frozen in the inkwells on their desks in the morning. Every week the children were checked for lice by the school nurses. My mother dreaded these visits, despite the fact that the nurses told her how clean and silky her hair was. Boys had to shave their heads altogether.

Every morning, at the same hour, interrupting whatever the class was doing, be it a quiz or a dictation, ladies in immaculately clean, starched white aprons came into the classroom carrying trays with a piece of sugar and a piece of rye bread or a small bagel for each student. These were free for schoolchildren to supplement the food rations. They were not something to scoff at and were eagerly anticipated.

The rationing system would be abolished in December 1947, but until then, since practically half of the country lay in ruins after the war, bread, butter, sugar, soap and some other items were gotten for monthly coupons, distributed to each member of the family. The biggest scare of those years was to lose the coupons, which could mean death by hunger. The coupons were not replaceable. There was an alternative. People could buy food in special stores at so-called "commercial" prices, but few families could afford the cost on a regular basis. Once, after having pawned one of her better pieces of clothing, as she often did to supplement her husband's salary, Olga bought a small pastry from one of these stores to treat her son, who was still a preschooler and happened to be with her. After every minuscule bite, to prolong the pleasure, the little boy would say, in a shaky voice, "We should leave a piece for my sister," until Olga promised to buy her daughter one, to appease his conscience.

In order to graduate from high school and get the Certificate of Secondary Education, also called a "maturity certificate," students had to pass the examinations, which included an essay on Russian literature and a written test in mathematics. My mother had always been a straight-5 student, but unexpectedly got a 4 on her final Russian literature essay exam. She had made no mistakes, but her handwriting and the overall presentation (she had a few corrections) were deemed inadequate for a gold medal. The rules were strict. My mother got a silver medal, as my father did, but was devastated by the fact. Her despair had almost cost her a higher education degree.

Helen Trepelkov

On September 1, when practically all her schoolmates hurried happily to various institutes, my mother sat at home. She had applied to MGIMO—she had already met my father by that time and liked what he told her about his studies—but on bad luck's roll, or maybe just badly shaken and having lost her self-assurance, she got a 4 for Russian dictation. It was time, however, for the self-pitying stage to end. My mother mustered all of her courage and called the rector of the MGIMO. My mother recounted all her miseries in detail to the man. The rector must have been impressed by her guts, if not by her story, for he invited her for an interview. He allowed her to attend the classes without official student status, with the understanding that she had to earn only perfect grades at the winter examination session in order to become a bona fide student. She did.

***

My mother met my father on her seventeenth birthday, during the summer after ninth grade. She was playing volleyball in summer camp, and my father, who was already a student and had a summer job as a counselor in a boys' camp, had brought his charges to play volleyball with the girls' team. Two years later, my parents were married.

I had heard about Deanna Durbin since I was a young child. Her movies came to the Soviet Union through the land-lease channels and as war trophies. Everybody in my family loved her, including my father. He had told me many times about her, especially about the movie, *His Butler's Sister*, where she sung Russian romances. I have always assumed that he just liked the popular actress of his youth, whose movies he saw for the first time as a very young man while working in Germany after the war. When I saw my father for the last time, two months before he died, he mentioned Deanna Durbin again. He told me how my mother had the exact same hairdo in her youth, and one front strand of her hair fell exactly the way Deanna Durbin's did.

Sometime later, I read a short paragraph in small print in *Time* magazine about Deanna Durbin's death at the age of 91. My heart sank when I saw the familiar name in the Milestones section. To me, it was more than the passing of a human being. It was the end of an era.

Postgraduate Studies in Motherhood

A few years after her marriage, my mother would transfer to the Moscow State University and graduate *summa cum laude*. She received a few very tempting job offers upon graduation. Yet, after weighing all the pros and cons of her familial situation, she became a stay-at-home mom and housewife. Due to my father's disruptive overseas assignments and the added stress of having to provide what my parents considered adequate care for my brother and myself, she practically had no way to squeeze in a career. The decision was made a little easier by the fact that such a lifestyle was much more in keeping with the times than it is now. My brother and I, and our father by the same token, were only the happier for it. She has always been very proud of having been recognized, but she has never regretted her choice. Children are good at sensing these things. I would have known.

Once, quite unsuspectingly, I provided my mother with a validation of sorts for her decision.

I was playing with my friends at a country house we had rented during one of the summers of my early childhood, and the kids were teasing me for being dressed too warmly on a rather hot day, which, quite frankly, I was. My grandmother, who happened to pass by at that time, overheard me telling them that my mother graduated from Moscow University, and she knew how to dress me.

So by the age of seven, when Russian children started school at the time, I already held education in high esteem.

Chapter Eight

Despite all the attention to intellectual fare, feeding children was a very serious business in our family when I was growing up. A lot of time and effort went into it. So, not surprisingly, I started paying close attention to our daughters' nutrition long before I began devising ways to attend to their spiritual health and development. I firmly adhered to the principle that we are what we eat and was monitoring their diets scrupulously. It was the only sacred area I rarely made any concessions in. Yet, shamefully, one of Nathalie's first words was *cookie*. If it was not really her first word, it certainly was one of her favorites. One of my good friends was a great cook, and while it was impossible to catch Lydia to feed her anything while she was driving at breakneck speed on her Mickey Mouse tricycle, my friend would often treat Nathalie, still a baby in my arms, with one of her scrumptious creations. I did not have the heart to say no.

Both my grandmother and my mother cooked all the meals. There was no such thing as fast food in the Soviet Union of my childhood. With very few exceptions, for the vast majority, if one wanted to eat, one had to cook. To this day, I remember the many mouthwatering concoctions I ate at my house and at the houses of my family and friends. The ladies were perfect at the craft. Their creativity and resourcefulness were absolutely fantastic, and I'm pretty sure many of them would have made even the Michelin-star honored institutions proud.

There were glitches sometimes, however. Shortly after my brother was born, my parents bought an apartment in a beautiful new district of Moscow. There were no supermarkets in the Soviet Union, so usually one had to visit several stores to buy all the groceries one needed. There was a specialized fish store very close to our building. The store carried live fish, and so one fine day my grandmother came to visit us carrying a huge kicking bundle. She often brought us food considering my father was away at that time and it was not easy for my mother to grocery shop with a huge baby carriage. It turned out to be a live catfish. Immediately, our bathtub was filled with water, and the fish swam there comfortably. As it turned out soon enough, my grandmother overestimated her ability to handle live victuals. The fish was never killed. What became of it is still a mystery, at least to me, but I wouldn't put it past my grandmother to have carried it late at night to the Moscow River nearby and set it free. At least I like to think this is what she did, and that the fish found its way to wherever it needed to be in the unpolluted waters of the sixties of the last century.

I loved my mother's cooking the best. She had always been a stickler as far as nutrition was concerned. She was truly obsessed with healthy eating habits. She would wash the fruit and vegetables several times, throwing away any product that even remotely looked or smelled suspicious to her. She was strongly against mayonnaise, cold cuts, any processed food in general, and would never dream of serving anything marinated in vinegar. She had a manicure only if she absolutely had to, usually when she had a reception to attend, lest chips of the nail polish fall into our food. Throughout our childhood, breakfast meant oatmeal, farmer's cheese, or yogurt. This delicate tender lady held us in check for many years as we had to comply with draconian rules regarding the quality of what went into our mouths. This task was made easier by the fact that whatever she cooked was delicious. Very often my father, who loved a good meal, would say at dinner, "Mom is a great cook, isn't she?" and my brother and I, our mouths full, would happily nod our heads in consent.

My mother is a great cook, but she has never been a cordon bleu chef. What is her secret? When my own daughters were growing up, Lydia introduced a new term, "cooked with love."

"Oh, Mom, this is really cooked with love," she told me once after dinner. I took her culinary remarks quite seriously after she amazed me in the sixth grade by picking up on a minuscule amount of nutmeg I had added to one of my dishes. Love indeed can make a difference. I am sure that is exactly what set my mother's cooking apart. The meals of my childhood just had a special magic to them. I am a great believer in TLC.

I had an occasional dalliance with something really bad for me, however, at least what I perceived as really bad. Considering the strictness of my everyday diet, even the school cafeteria would usually fit the bill. I would order something fried—sausage, ideally—topped with heaps of mustard and mayo, and the guilty scrumptiousness of it would keep me going for a month or two. Two foods were allowed in unlimited quantities in our family, however. These were caviar and chocolate. Black caviar in Russia was readily available and relatively inexpensive when I was a preschooler. I loved it, and eating it came with an added bonus. I would ask my mother to save the empty glass containers for me to use as building blocks. I had dozens of them. Chocolate intake was never restricted either, especially when we were living in Switzerland. I took advantage of this with a vengeance. I am sure that I am hardly to blame, for few people could have resisted the temptation.

Interestingly enough, it was my father who gave me the most comprehensive cooking lesson of all. I was already in my twenties, about to be married. I came to visit him in Geneva, where he was posted at the time. My mother had some business to take care of in Moscow and was to join us a week or two later. My future husband was also there on a short business trip, and I decided to cook them both dinner. I planned, shopped, and cooked the whole meal myself. It looked like I had done a pretty good job and both men praised my efforts and seemed to genuinely enjoy it.

The next day, a Saturday, my father took me to the supermarket. He told me that there were some smart tricks to keep in mind while shopping. My guess was, judging by the amount of money I had spent on my celebratory dinner, my father realized that there was no way my prospective husband's salary could accommodate my shopping habits, and neither would his, on a regular basis. He explained to me that small quantities of the item cost relatively more than the larger ones, told me what made sense to buy on sale and what did not, how to plan a balanced menu to reduce waste, what combinations of cheeses to buy for a cheese plate, and many other tricks of the trade. The seed was planted. He had piqued my curiosity, or rather let me realize what a vast and challenging field homemaking could be, and most importantly, that I had a lot to learn.

Postgraduate Studies in Motherhood

***

Some people have a tendency to think too much. As my daughters cheerfully remind me on a daily basis, I am one of those people. I have always had, for better or worse, a propensity toward strategic thinking. I have always needed a strategy, not just random useful facts, in all of my undertakings.

I view it as an algorithm to attract certain knowledge to achieve a certain result. I can't just let life take its course, I need an active stance. At every turning point of my life I try to assess the situation, evaluate the facts, and only then make a decision. Life is really pure mathematics, in a way. I do not want to go left and right and back and forth, like a piece of wood in the sea, and lose both time and momentum. Studying vectors in school did not exactly reinforce this position, but rather supplied a graphic interpretation for it. I did not want to end up with an inch of forward movement at the end of the day. Gary Kasparov once said, "All chess players agree that a bad plan is better than no plan." I always need a plan, although chess is probably the only hobby of my father's that I did not adopt. As much as I enjoyed winning, the primary pleasure of any game for me was social interaction, and chess was too demanding to allow one to lose concentration.

My strategy, precisely, should not have trumped the happiness of everyday life. I had to know where I wanted to be, but also to have a blast getting there. One should not postpone life. I suspect that my need to always have a plan was originally rooted in my aversion to waste since I was a child. When we were living at the country house during one of my preschool summers, my five-year-old friend showed up one day with a gorgeous dahlia. She was obsessed with the flower for a few hours, but then she must have gotten tired of it, for toward the evening I saw this flower lying in the middle of the road, lifeless and forgotten, all dirty and flattened by human feet who were stepping on it in total disregard for its recent glory.

There was another, even earlier episode that left an equally deep mark. It happened the summer before my brother was born. My mother could not walk for many hours at a time, so we usually would go into the woods, find some fallen tree or stumps to sit on, and would have our lunch, which consisted of sandwiches with hard-cooked salami, which would be banned from our diets later on, but which I loved very much then, and still do.

I enjoyed one particular spot. It was a clearing in the woods entirely covered by bluebells. The color of those flowers is my favorite color to this day. No wonder I enjoyed that place. It was a rather secluded part of the forest, but once three people, two men and a woman, happened to pass by. They went straight through the clearing, leaving a trail of crushed flowers behind. As if this was not bad enough, the woman, without stopping, tore a huge amount of bluebells with one sweeping movement of her hand, without so much as looking at what she was doing. I was too young to conscientiously regret the ephemeral nature of physical beauty along the lines of *sic transit gloria mundi*. I just felt sorry for the beautiful flowers ravaged so carelessly and unnecessarily.

I never assumed that having a strategy automatically guaranteed success. It is not a silver bullet, far from it. Complacency is our worst enemy, we always have to make sure that our hand is still on the pulse, that our strategy is still valid. We have to be prepared to go back to square one at any given moment and start from scratch should we realize we've made a mistake. It does keep us on our toes. Who would have thought that being a stay-at-home mom could mean living so dangerously!

This brings back the memory of the housekeeping lessons of my childhood. When I was growing up, girls and boys had separate but rather substantial domestic education in school. As early as the first grade, girls were taught to sew on buttons—in cross and parallel stitching—different embroidery stitches, knitting, and mending. In sixth grade, we were taught how to sew a blouse. We made a pattern based on our measurements and had to sew it on a sewing machine. Boys were taught how to do handiwork around the house, from how to use a hammer to how to make a shelf. In the Swiss school, I had cooking lessons in the seventh or eighth grade.

Anyone who knits knows how annoying it is to notice you made a mistake many rows later. You face a painful dilemma. Either leave everything as it is, and have an imperfect sweater, scarf, or whatever (more likely than not no one will ever even notice) or undo the work, correct the mistake, lose a lot of time, but live happily ever after having satisfied your inner perfectionist. I do remember how strict our teachers were on this subject. And there was no chance *they* wouldn't notice! We had to undo the work every time. Interestingly, my mother remembers the same approach, too. It is truly amazing how seemingly unimportant, almost marginal skills could be used as a very powerful character-building tool.

I duly taught our girls to sew on buttons, but I must admit, it never really took. No wonder. I remember my shock when a few years ago I heard a young girl at the dry cleaners request a button be sewn on her pants. It was easier for her to take her pants to the dry cleaners than to do it herself! It took some time to sink in. She probably could not even do it herself! Times do change, indeed, we need different activities to make our point, but the character-building blocks are still there, not to be dismissed. We just have to find more appropriate examples. Maybe now it would involve the child's blog or web page?

I continued the search for my unique approach.

***

My relationship with the notables of pediatrics did not work out very well, alas, the first time around. The grand finale happened shortly after Nathalie was born. I don't remember now whether I read it in Dr. Spock's book or heard it on the popular Lifetime television program, *What Every Baby Knows,* by the famous Dr. T. Berry Brazelton, or maybe from some other source. It does not really matter. Nathalie was crying and it looked like she had colic. The advice was to put the colicky baby in a baby chair and place the chair on top of a working dishwasher. The vibration of the machine was supposed to soothe the baby. It did not work for Nathalie. After a few minutes of the agony that is a screaming baby on a rumbling dishwasher, I grabbed Nathalie and just did it the old-fashioned way; that is, I paced the room holding her tight against my heart until she calmed down. After that, the books were relegated to the farthest corner of my bookshelf.

At that time, I just didn't have the ability to sort and process various bits of knowledge from different sources. I did not know where to place them, how to pigeonhole them, so they just rolled off me for the most part, like water off a duck's back. I felt like the blindfolded person in a game of

Pin the Tail on the Donkey. I was turning in the dark, and kept missing my mark. The human being has to be ready to accept knowledge as the soil has to be prepared to accept the grain. Clearly I was not quite ready yet. Of course I did not think I knew everything there was to know about raising children. On the contrary, the vastness of the field, my complete ignorance of the subject, and the scarcity of free time to get and process information made me both skeptical and wary.

As a person used to studying, I usually knew exactly when I had reached the precious moment of having grasped the inner workings, the inner logic of the subject, with all the facts falling neatly into place. Only then could I believe in myself and trust my judgment. I knew very well that I was far from that point, and was instinctively shying away from the new terrain, relying instead on the primordial instinct of maternal love and the maternal intuition, as much as on good old common sense. In other words, doing pretty much to the letter what Doctor Spock and Doctor Brazelton advised, as I found out a few years later.

First, I had to define myself. Then I could come up with a conception of my own. My strategy had to be hard won by trial and error. It could not come fresh from a book, it had to come from within, and it had to be mine. To put it simply, first I had to understand what motherhood meant to me and define my goals as far as raising my children was concerned.

This is a very trivial comparison, but I feel it is the same with clothes, or home design. If you have a strong idea of your style, you won't be tempted to buy those shoes just because they are marked seventy-five percent off the manufacturer's suggested price, or bring home some incongruous item from your next trip. To wander safely, you have to be properly moored.

The process had already begun however, in some parallel tracks of my mind, even as I was putting the books away. When Alex was home and I knew I did not have to worry about Lydia, I would often put Nathalie on my belly after each feeding and gently stroke her head, unwilling to let go of my precious bundle. Once, when she was not even two weeks old, I was enjoying the same routine. I stopped for a few moments, distracted by something. When I looked back at Nathalie, I saw her head slowly coming up. It was still so week, it swayed a little from side to side. Like a sunflower turning its beautiful head toward the sun, my daughter was making a conscientious effort to follow my loving hand. When I picked up the books for the second time when Nathalie was a toddler and reread about the need to listen to my baby and show her my love, I knew exactly where to pin it.

Most of my own parental insights came to me in the shower or while I was doing the dishes. This is very understandable, considering those were about the only two activities that allowed me to think. My thoughts more often than not had little novelty in them, and the amount of wheels I reinvented could have very well outfitted a long freight train. Anyway, one of such spontaneous revelations was the thought that the world around us is beautiful and needs to be presented to the girls in all its glory.

Well, maybe not that spontaneous. Like many people, I mused over the meaning of life now and then. I believe that this is one of the most personal questions, and probably there are as many meanings as there are people. My epiphany came when I was once quite randomly watching a nonfiction movie about conception and childbirth. In a very realistic simulation on the screen you could see a large egg bombarded by dozens of spermatozoa. I realized back then that never is this fight for life more intense, more desperate, and more terminal than at this hidden moment when the beginning of one life means the end before even a chance at a beginning for so many others. I felt that we all were those few chosen ones who drew the lucky ticket.

And this is what life is to me. It is a precious gift—a gift to walk this earth after so many others who lived, before so many more yet to come, and an even greater number of those who did not get a chance at life. I am happy and grateful, and I try never to lose this perspective.

The more I thought about it, the more my approach shaped up and acquired a practical rationale as well. Funny how little things lead sometimes to generalizations with great impact. Once, when we were driving through Switzerland, we had not familiarized ourselves enough with our itinerary and we missed some very interesting festival or something of the sort within just a couple of miles off our route. Ignorance, I reasoned, equaled missed opportunities. On the other hand, I wanted the girls to be ready for anything life threw at them.

As I lived and learned myself, I became more and more aware of the need to prepare the soil in advance for the knowledge to take root.

Helen Trepelkov

Examples of this quality of the learning process, big and small, were all around me, starting with my double take at child-raising staples.

Early on I noticed how a reference to some foreign city or a work of art makes any book I read much more interesting and makes a greater impression if I can picture what the author is talking about. A word the meaning of which I just looked up in the dictionary kept popping up almost every day from then on. A piece of pottery I first saw in some remote Thai village seemed to have moved back to New York with me by some uncanny power and became ubiquitous, as if by magic, staring at me from literally every Broadway stall. Coincidences? I don't think so. I just never noticed, never registered what I did not understand or what I was not familiar with. I did not want our daughters to travel through life the same way, looking without seeing, listening but not hearing. I wanted them to be at home with as many things, places, skills, and concepts as possible, and to learn the value of things around them all along the way. This desire was reinforced as I saw the concept of thinking outside the box being promoted. I figured nothing helped as much as seeing the big picture.

There was an accident that really made me pay attention. You could say I learned the hard way. We were exploring a new playground. Lydia was five and Nathalie was two. It was a chilly winter day, and we had the whole area to ourselves. I took this chance to relax a little and sat down, which I rarely did if there were many kids around. Lydia jumped at the opportunity to use the swing. Our usual playground did not have any. She was going pretty high and was obviously having a great time. In the beginning, Nathalie was more interested in the slide, but seeing how much fun Lydia was having, she must have changed her mind, because all of a sudden she darted straight for the swing. It was made of a solid wood board, with a metal reinforcement along the perimeter.

My blood chilled in my veins. I ran to cut her off but she was too far away and I didn't have time. It all happened in less than a minute. The swing hit Nathalie and propelled her a few yards forward. When I finally grabbed her, I could not believe how lucky we were. The swing hit her straight in the recess under her lower lip, and the down winter jacket softened her fall. There was a hospital right across the street, and we left with just a Band-Aid a few minutes later. After my terror gave way to surprise, and I started analyzing the incident, I thought, *how could a kid, who was smart enough to know better, do such a thing?* She knew she had to stay away from moving things. The only explanation I could come up with was that having never seen a swing before Nathalie had no idea what to expect from it. I learned my lesson. It also reinforced my desire to expose the girls to as many life experiences as possible.

Still, at first it was an impulse. I wanted to give our daughters the world, I wanted them to see how exciting and exhilarating life is, so they would not waste theirs when they grew up. I wanted them to see, to hear, to smell, to touch, and to taste as much as possible. At that point, when they were still preschoolers, I wanted them mostly to absorb, to take in. To be able, when they grew up, to stop in their tracks and enjoy the human genius and a melody at Carnegie Hall, or the solemn beauty of a winter forest, or their own mastery and strength while swimming along some rugged coastline, or making pirouettes under the watchful eye of Prometheus on the Rockefeller Center ice-skating rink. And, incidentally, to know who Prometheus was. I wanted them to learn to love and to celebrate life. I wanted to teach them to be happy. This is when the best time of my life officially began.

Chapter Nine

My parents did not make any attempts to teach me to read or write until I turned seven in March and was about to start school in the fall of that year. It was my father who would try to prepare me for school. It was an absolute disaster and didn't last for more than a few sessions. My father was not a very patient man, and I was stubborn, and frankly not very interested. Other brief episodes influenced me more than those explicit attempts at formal education. I still remember some of them as vividly as if it was yesterday.

Once my father was rocking me on his foot, which I liked a lot (I must have been about five at the time). Suddenly he stopped and told me that girls didn't ride in this manner, that I should sit aside, with both legs on the same side, rather than astride. He rose, went to his study, and very carefully picked up an old art book, its glossy pages smelling of old paper, glue, and typographic paint. He showed me reproductions of some beautiful paintings with ladies mounting horses in the feminine fashion. He made his point, of course. But more importantly, I became forever fascinated by the almost religious ritual of holding and consulting a great book. This episode took place more than fifty years ago and didn't last for more than ten minutes, but I still remember the smell of the old pages and the feeling of conspiracy and enunciation to some breathtaking and beautiful secret.

It was also my father who introduced me to hobbies and explained to me the idea and the meaning of the word the summer before I started school. He told me that I should always have an interest outside my job. The timing was not accidental, since school was always considered an equivalent of the children's work in our family, and my responsibility as a family member was to study. So much so, that I was never asked to do any household chores.

It wasn't that I didn't want to help, when I was a child myself. I would not blame my parents, however, if they were secretly more prepared to pay me to stay away, and that only the outrageous impropriety, from the pedagogical point of view, of such an attitude made them reluctantly accept my contributions.

I was very eager from a very early age. We even had our own *Groundhog Day* episode in the family when I was four. When my grandmother would come to visit us, she would often bring the dough and a jar of jam for a quick pie. Every single time I would snatch this glass jar and run to the bathroom to wash it, since I couldn't reach the faucet in the kitchen. More often than not, I would drop the jar and sit quietly afterward while my mother and grandmother would clean up the mess.

My father would have none of this "resigned to the unavoidable" kind of attitude and had a different approach to my obsession with carrying things. We were walking home one day when we saw watermelons on sale in the street. We stopped to get one. I volunteered to carry it. My father told me it was too heavy for me, and I would most likely drop it. I was four years old. I insisted. Then he proposed an agreement. He would let me carry it, but if I dropped it, we would not get another one. I was very confident and sure of myself (on what grounds, I have no idea) and agreed. I dropped the watermelon. I stuck to my end of the deal, and we proceeded home in silence. A bargain is a bargain. I was too proud to ask for clemency. I felt extremely disappointed, but not so much at not getting to eat a watermelon. I was very disappointed that I failed at my task.

The culmination of my zeal, however, was my attempt to wash a chicken with soap. Back then, chickens were sold whole, with legs and head intact, with a limp crest and murky rolled eyes. It was usually held over the gas flame of the stove to eliminate the few random unplucked feathers, and the smell of burnt flesh lingered in the apartment for quite some time after the procedure.

I think that finally did it. I was denied access to food items from then on.

Yet I never felt any annoyance emanating from my mother. She loved us and loved taking care of us, and this feeling ultimately shaped my attitude toward housework. I feel that when you love someone you want to take care of that person. It is a pleasure, not a burden.

This is why I never liked the word "chores" in the family context. I remembered how much loving care went into my mother's homemaking, all the big and small testimonies of her love, and how special just being home felt for me. I wanted to do the same for my husband and our girls. I knew that education went beyond our pointed attempts and that children don't learn from what they are told as much as what they see. I did not want our girls to learn house chores. I wanted to teach them to feel and appreciate this tender magic of love and to learn to take care of those they love, too, when their turn came.

***

The summer before I started school, my father suggested that I could begin collecting plants for a herbarium. When the casually suggested activity took root, I received a great atlas of plants from our region that my father bought in an antiquarian bookstore. It was a large book, bound in what must have once been a nice deep green, but by that time had become a faded yellowish fabric.

My mother was not a fan of old books. My grandmother's youngest brother, Boris, succumbed to tuberculosis in 1960, at the age of 33. When he was in the hospital, Olga would spend many hours with him, helping the hospital staff to cook, to feed him and his roommates, and to clean the facility. After those visits, she would take long showers disinfecting every inch of her body before returning to her family. I remember my grandmother whispering his name after his death over and over again, and crying.

I was the only one of her grandchildren to be allowed to call her Olia, a diminutive from the formal Olga. Once, shortly after Boris died, my grandmother and I were alone in the house. I was two years old. She started crying, as she often did at that time when she was alone with me. She probably thought I was too young to understand what was going on. I was, but I did realize that she was very unhappy. As I was told later, I called her Olia, as I heard everybody call her, and hugged her in an effort to comfort her. I have been calling her Olia ever since.

Tuberculosis was still a very real threat at the time, and doctors warned that the infection could live in books for years. The personal tragic

81

encounter with the disease made my mother very acutely aware of the fact.

But I had to have the atlas. A shaky compromise was found. I remember my grandmother ironing every page, all two to three hundreds of them, in order to disinfect the book.

This hobby lasted for almost five years and was joined and subsequently replaced by a vivid interest in animals. Again, a plethora of great books. Six wonderful, huge volumes, the world of animals. Many other hobbies followed. The main supplier of ideas and the promoter of the concept was, of course, my father. He introduced me to numismatics and I got my first camera as a birthday gift when I turned 11.

My father was not one to be deterred by difficulties, he was exhilarated by opportunities. And opportunities we took. He was not afraid to try new things, have new experiences, and entrained all his family with him. I was his most enthusiastic follower. To this day, I need to have a hobby and I love collecting things. Whether it made me a more interesting person or increased my market value is open to debate, but it certainly made my life a much more fascinating affair.

He was always trying to share his omnifarious interests with me. He was the one who took me to the planetarium when I was six. I was fascinated by a huge replica of the moon, with all the mountain ranges and ocean beds, and one sector totally smooth. As my father explained, that was the invisible side of the moon, no data as to its terrain was available at that time. I remembered that trip when looking at the picture of the first man on the moon on the front cover of the *Paris Match* magazine less than ten years later.

I was about seven years old when my father solemnly told me that maybe I would be interested in collecting stamps, and brought me to the philatelist section of the bookstore. I was thrilled. All those stamps in long neat rows, walls of stamps. He told me there were so many stamps that I should narrow down my collection to one topic. I found some big San Marino ones with gorgeous colorful butterflies on them that I loved. My father explained to me the meaning of the term "flora and fauna," and we decided to go with it.

I would sit at my father's desk and flip through the pages of the stamp albums. These small colorful pieces of paper with beautiful pictures and unfamiliar and mysterious letters on them were like windows to equally unfamiliar and mysterious worlds. They fascinated me. I learned the Latin alphabet in order to be able to read the names of the countries. I would read them aloud, and the very sound of those words made me physically experience the huge distance to those faraway lands. I immediately decided that I had mastered the English language.

My eagerness needs a little clarification. There were two major types of schools in the Soviet Union at that time: regular ones, where studying foreign language began in the fifth grade (the first year of middle school) and the specialized schools, where the study of foreign language started as early as the second grade. By that time, English had already substituted German as the most studied foreign language in Russian schools. I was attending a regular school just across the street and was more than a little jealous of the kids from our building who were attending the English specialized ones. Their proud parents would often help their kids do their English assignments outside on the benches on warm evenings, speaking loudly and clearly, so that the humble hoi polloi in the proximity (including me) had no doubt that it was English spoken there, indeed.

It took me a few days to realize my mistake. The revelation occurred when I decided that, having mastered reading, I should move on to writing, my idea being to write Russian words using Latin letters. Reading them aloud made me realize that I was definitely missing something.

Many children from our building not only studied English in school, but also attended musical schools after regular classes. Our family was hopelessly not musical. My father liked to sing in the shower on weekends, and I'm afraid that was the extent of his musical accomplishments. As for my mother...she liked to read poems aloud as a child. She did it extremely well, and without fail took part in all the school concerts and even in a big charity event in Stockholm once, on par with adults. So, when the time came to grade her singing efforts in junior school, the teacher said, referring to her reading skills, "Sing you cannot, and that's a fact, but you have a true God's gift," and gave her the highest grade.

I had never shown any promise with music either. That is not to say that this staple of a traditional education was not paid due attention. When I was six years old, my father took me for an audition. I had never bothered to ask what kind of musical institution it was. I remember a big stark room with a black grand piano in the center as its only piece of furniture and a severe lady in a dark dress and high heels. I have absolutely no recollection of what I was asked to do, but whatever it was, I must have pitifully failed, for there was no follow up to this musical overture. I took music lessons for a few years later, however, with a private teacher in Moscow and in a musical school in Geneva. The forbidden fruit obsessed me, and my parents gave way to my persistent nagging.

My brief career in sports had the same deplorable outcome. All such classes involved some sort of commute, making it very hard for my mother to take me, considering my brother was just a toddler at the time. The last winter before I started school, my indefatigable father found some evening figure skating classes not far from our house. Twice a week, I would skate on a small outdoor rink in our local park, bathed in the glow of powerful lights encircling the rink, the only bright spot amid the complete darkness of the park. Enthusiastic parents would wait at the edge, a warm squirmy mass against the frozen stillness of the backdrop. My father, like all the other parents, would stand there, stomping his feet and rubbing his hands together in a vain attempt to keep warm, or else blowing on them, and small white puffs of vapor would immediately crystallize into shimmering frost on his eyelashes and eyebrows.

I was not great. I got just one "good" grade, for my "shoot the duck" move, in a steady stream of "satisfactory" ones. I was impervious to the teasing and mildly offensive remarks of the teacher, who called one of my efforts at a spiral a "sparrow on ice," but this last remark probably did it for my father. These sessions stopped, without my taking any notice.

***

My father did start me on reading, though. One fine day he just brought home and put in front of me the book, *Osceola the Seminole*. Thomas Mayne Reid, Fenimore Cooper, Sir Walter Scott, Robert Stevenson, Jules Verne. I fell under the spell of these books about faraway lands. The enchanting world of adventure still has a firm grip on me. Riding a wild mustang in an endless prairie with the wind in my hair and my face became my dream. I think the dream did come true, in its tamest version and suitably adjusted to modern times, thirty years later, when I was regularly driving from New York City to DC to visit our daughters when they were studying at Georgetown University.

My father loved books. All his life he regretted that he had to sell some of his late grandfather's beautiful, leather-bound volumes when he was a student. He lived with his grandmother at that time. He was already in his late twenties, and felt shy about asking his parents for money. It was just not done. He felt it was his turn to help them at that point. The education in the Soviet Union, including higher education, was free, and Soviet college students were even paid a monthly stipend to allow those without parental support or other financial means to continue their studies. His stipend and various odd jobs that he took to supplement it, mostly lecturing, were sometimes not enough to cover his expenses.

Books had been equally venerated in my mother's house. Books were a luxury back then. As with most consumer goods, they were in short supply. On top of that, after the war, my relatives had other vital needs to satisfy and spend their modest means on. My mother got a wonderful special edition of Pushkin (his 150th anniversary was celebrated in 1949), which her father managed to find when she turned 15. The same year, for his tenth birthday, her brother got a huge tome of Belinsky, a famous literary critic of the nineteenth century, spotted by my grandmother at the local thrift market. It was actually my mother's doing. She was accompanying my grandmother that day, and swiftly promised to add her Swedish skis to the gift if her mother got the book. The book was bought and read by my mother, and her brother enjoyed my mother's treasured skis. All the love for books could not have made my mother part with her Swedish ice skates, however. Those were the real McCoy, genuine hockey blades, not some girly figure-skating ones. She used to wear them when ice-skating with her dad in Sweden on winter Sundays. She recalls those outings very vividly to this day. She was bursting with pride, for she thought her dad was the most handsome, graceful, and masterful man on the rink. These books still hold a special place among our family heirlooms.

I loved listening to my grandmother Olga and my uncle talking about literature. I read many wonderful books at their suggestion, mostly Russian classics, which they both knew almost by heart. My grandmother also introduced me to Stephan Zweig, who is one of my favorite writers to this day. My uncle even recommended a couple of books in English. He self-taught English in his forties, in order to read foreign publications on engineering.

It was my mother who suggested I read *The Gadfly*, which would become my favorite. A storm of feelings, an anthology of betrayal. Love and betrayal. The eternal duo, clasped together in a precarious equilibrium, bound to falter for as long as man exists.

Interestingly enough, with my affinity for abstract reasoning, my feelings of love were always very specific. I never tried to bring good to the whole world, but to create a small oasis of happiness. Although I always tried to set only the highest standards as far as my children were concerned, my ambitions were not to have the best children, but to give them the best.

This is why our girls attended one of the best musical schools as preschoolers, a painting class organized by the retired head of an art school on the premises of an art museum attended mostly by children of painters and art critics, and a ballet-on-ice group oriented toward prospective professional training.

I was positive that those who aim higher go further. Such goal-setting gave me a better sense of direction and perspective. It did not mean that I would achieve that perfection, only that no matter how far I went, the movement would be in the right direction, and I would get as close to it as I possibly could, not losing time on back roads and wayward ways.

***

As time passed, my spontaneous desire to make our daughters enjoy the world around them blended seamlessly with the desire to make them learn all about the world to prepare them for their life in it. Before they were old enough to understand its laws through science, I wanted them to perceive them through its harmony, through its beauty. To understand and appreciate beauty not only makes our lives fuller and more interesting, but also helps align them along the cosmic laws.

Human society to me is like an orchestra. Everyone is playing his or her own melody, with a certain amount of sharps or flats in it. Cosmic harmony is governing the music-making process, but we are free to choose our melody. How atrociously boring life would be if everybody played the same note on the same instrument! The important thing is not to play falsely. Before expecting our girls to produce any melody of their own, however, I wanted to help them prepare their instrument and tune it to the world's harmony in order to be part of the orchestra. This makes one at peace with oneself, proud to belong, and strong with collective strength.

My idea, crystal clear at last, was not to make a perfect musician, a perfect painter, or a perfect sportsman, but rather to develop to the maximum the girls' ability to perceive the world through our senses, to achieve perfect human pitch and great width and depth of perception.

I respect the collective intelligence of people, be it popular wisdom or religious values. Previous generations knew a thing or two about raising children, I figured. This is why, without much ado, I opted for the time-honored old-fashioned ways: painting, piano lessons, and sports. And of course, reading. I was so thrilled, so impatient. I was also very methodical. I wanted to stimulate and develop the mind, the senses, and the body. I went into my new venture with a vengeance.

Reading allows us to hone our own values and principles by pitching them against the concentrated experiences of other people, and by exposing us to all the wisdom of previous generations at our own pace, in the privacy of our own homes. In a way, reading is like a life test drive, a life simulator.

I also felt that our daughters were deprived to a great extent of the advantages of growing up in an extended family. When we are young, we mostly give our children our strength, when we are middle-aged, we give our children our friendship, and when we are old, we give our children our wisdom. Growing up amid people of different ages allows one to have it all at the same time. Growing up in an extended family also gives you a certain insight into your future. Reading could partially fill this gap.

Having never attended any preschool institutions, I was steeped instead in the relationships with my numerous relatives, my early outlook on life shaped by personal interactions with those I knew and countless stories about those I did not.

My only stint at daycare was very short-lived. I did not like it. I wanted to be home with my mom. I was distracted from my unhappiness for the first three days, because my joining the group coincided with the arrival of new bikes for the children. They were not just plain childish tricycles, they had two big shiny wheels and just two small supporting ones at each side of the back ones. When I grew tired of riding the bikes, I stopped saying hello to the teacher, she couldn't take it, and that was the end of it. With this memory in mind, I assumed that our girls were bound to hate daycare, too, and was prepared to fight tooth and nail to keep the girls at home. As a result, our children were denied a chance to upkeep the family tradition of snubbing their nose at the venerable institution. But Nathalie, when she was about four years old, walked out once during a theater performance. She got scared when the big bad wolf was about to have dinner, and decided not to witness the act. I barely caught up with her in the lounge.

Lydia's attitude toward school has always been positive, but temperate. Nathalie, on the other hand, loved school to the point of crying when she got the chickenpox in the spring of her first grade and had to miss a few days for the first time in her school career. Whether it shows that she would have been very happy in daycare or that I was right to wait until she was mature enough for a childcare institution, I don't know. It could have worked out either way.

Chapter Ten

I had fun growing up. I really liked my relatives and enjoyed their company. We had quite a motley family, and I came to appreciate each one of them in their own right, for very different reasons. They came from various social backgrounds and lived in various locations. They presented quite an abundance of lifestyles, opinions, and convictions. We had the whole spectrum, from a daughter of a marshal of nobility in one of the cities on the Volga River to a Red Army soldier, awarded red revolutionary pants for his bravery.

During the difficult years of the Civil War, red soldiers were often awarded practical items, like clothing, for their bravery and other exploits. There was no unified uniform in the Red Army. Up until 1922, old military uniforms from the storage facilities all over Russia were used. These facilities carried, among other things, red pants for the tsarist cavalry men. They became an award for the Red Army soldiers for outstanding military feats. "Red revolutionary pants," as they came to be known, were a rare award, and those who had them stood out in the crowd and had special privileges. The pants even came with a special certificate, to avoid fraud, my maternal grandmother told me. The brave soldier was her maternal uncle.

She also remembered the impeccably chiseled profile of her maternal Aunt Alexandra's aristocratic mother-in-law and her straight back, despite advanced age, as she was commenting on a funeral procession in the street. "Look, Alexandra, they are burying your Gorky," the lady said. This woman never accepted Soviet Russia and one of its greatest writers, Maxim Gorky. Her husband was the general manager of one of the big Moscow factories. He was an English engineer invited to work in Russia before the revolution. Their older children lived in England, but their two younger sons, Alexandra's husband, Andrey, and Vladimir, lived in Moscow with their parents. Andrey would become a prominent graphic artist. He would illustrate more than 200 books during his lifetime, mostly children's books.

His works are exhibited in many major Russian museums, among them the State Tretyakov Gallery and the Pushkin Museum. Vladimir, her youngest son, would be killed in 1941 as a member of the Moscow Militia, a voluntary formation of Moscow residents to defend the city during World War II, referred to as the Great Patriotic War in Russia.

This same unyielding woman was the one who helped Alexandra and her two young daughters the most when they lived in evacuation. Alexandra lost her first three children, three boys, in the early twenties. They froze to death in the maternity ward. Winters were cold in Moscow, and there was practically no fuel. More than three years of World War I, the Revolution, and the subsequent Russian Civil War took their toll.

My grandmother and her brother Leonid, as the oldest children who were already attending high school in Moscow, would sometimes manage to skip the watchful eye of their grandmother and come live with their young aunt and her new family for some time. Every morning, the building's street cleaner would start the oven, while Alexandra's father-in-law would go out to buy a warm loaf of bread, and the whole family would have hot tea with fresh bread and butter. Dinner meant homemade meatballs, their heavenly meat aroma much more effective at gathering the family around the dinner table than any dinner gong. The frequent exception was Vladimir, who would often come later at night, and his mother would then discreetly feed her youngest boy in the kitchen.

Alexandra loved her nieces and nephews her entire long life, trying to soften the blow of her older sister's untimely death for her nephews and nieces for more than forty years. .She died in her nineties. She had graduated from a gymnasium for girls and had taught Russian language and literature all her life. Tall, lean, straight, delicate, but strong by necessity, incurably romantic, with the same small briefcase carrying children's homework to correct every night, and a beautiful voice singing Russian romances to a grateful crowd of her older relatives and friends, much to the horror of the children, for to them it invariably meant utmost boredom. The last time we stayed in her country house for a few weeks with her daughters and their children was when she was already in her late eighties.

As with most people who knew what hunger was, she paid particular attention to our being well fed. It was a blessed late summertime with its bacchanalia of colors, aromas, and tastes, and she made sure we got a plentiful supply of fruit and vegetables from her small plot. My last memory of her is of her slowly and solemnly presiding over the tea ceremony, fighting with determination the start of a treacherous shaking of her hands.

***

The family lived right across from the Institute of Red Professors. Their house was demolished many years ago, but the building of the Institute still stands and has a special significance for our family. Before the Russian Revolution of 1917, it housed the Moscow Imperial Lyceum in memory of Tsarevich Nicholas (informally known as Katkovsky Lyceum), a privileged institution of higher education for the children of noble families. In fact, the building was constructed especially with this lyceum in view. My paternal grandfather was a student of this lyceum. In the early fifties, my parents studied in the very same building, only by then it already housed the Moscow State Institute for International Relations. My brother and I graduated from the same institute. Three generations attended courses in the same auditoriums, walked up the same stairs, holding the same rails.

The diversity of our family never troubled me or made me uncomfortable. On the contrary, it delighted me. Seeing each and every one of my relatives was rife with various opportunities for great fun. I loved collecting things since I can remember, and my family members were probably, in a way, my first collection.

Such social variety was common in Russia at that time. The 1917 Russian Revolution tossed the neatly layered society of Tsarist Russia as if by huge salad servers, and set the whole country in motion. The social Brownian movement became quickly polarized along the new major axis of Reds and Whites, creating an immense thrust at the scale of a huge country. The pitiless new force destroyed the old social structures, alienating friends, tearing apart family members. People who would have never met prior to the revolution had to live and work side by side. They became friends, they married. Not all of those unions lasted, the most random ones fell apart, but many endured. Painfully, slowly, a new social fabric was being woven; a new Russia was being born.

We used to see people often, visiting them or having them over practically every Sunday. Saturday was a working day back then. It was a time when not every family had a telephone in their apartment. It meant no one really knew when friends or family might show up on their doorstep.

My paternal great-grandmother was the oldest member of my family I have met. Everybody called her simply Grandma. When Vladimir, the oldest son in a respectable and affluent family, decided to marry a remarkably beautiful but poor girl of common background, my father's great-grandfather was adamant. When the defiant son finally married her in spite of all the familial resistance, he was practically shunned and stopped communicating with his family. Vladimir came to live in Moscow at the end of the nineteenth century from a city bordering Poland called Brest (Brest-Litovsk at the time). One of his ancestors, a military man, serving probably in the border forces, a commoner, made a brilliant military career, became a general, and was granted nobility for his outstanding service. He had no estates, however. Vladimir died when my father was only four years old.

His wife outlived him by more than thirty years. I vaguely remember a small, thin old lady dressed in all dark clothes with big tired hands crossed on her belly and piercingly blue eyes, still full of spirit. She had five sons and three daughters, my grandfather, Pavel, being the oldest.

She still lived in her old house with one of her sons, my father's uncle, Nikolai, and his family. It was the house where she had lived with her husband all her life and where she gave birth to all eight of her children. This was the house where my father was born, too. I liked to visit it. It was in the center of Moscow, and when in the early sixties it had to be demolished to give way to new high-rises, my father took me there to see it one last time, looking so forlorn in its imposed emptiness, to say good-bye.

Grandma died in the very beginning of the year I was about to turn four. My mother still likes to remember that when we saw her for the last time on New Year's Day, she told my mother that the girl (meaning me) was nice, but now my mother needed a son, too. Nine months later, almost to the day, my brother was born.

My grandfather Pavel left his part of the house to his younger brother, Nikolai, when he got married, and went to live with his wife, my grandmother, in the south of Russia after the Great Patriotic War. For that reason, I did not see them often. My paternal grandmother, Nadejda, was an orphan. Her parents, of noble origins, perished during the Revolution. It was the time when people with noble roots were looked upon with great suspicion, so she did not encourage talking about her past and never told us what happened. She was raised by her aunt, her mother's sister, and her husband, in their estate near the Russian city of Orel. Her cousins were taking music lessons, and my grandmother learned to play piano, too. This skill proved very useful. She used to work as a music teacher in daycare centers and schools that her children, two sons and one daughter, attended, to keep an eye on them.

My grandfather worked as an engineer at a plant. He was a very easygoing, happy person. My most vivid memory of him is that he was always aiming his camera at us. He developed his photos himself, and a couple of weeks after their visit we got dozens of pictures in the mail.

We used to see the younger uncle, Nikolai, the most. Nikolai was an engineer, as were all of his brothers. I don't know whether those were the times when every boy wanted to be an engineer, probably so, but I definitely had a lot of engineers in my family. Nikolai and his brother Dmitry were aviation engineers. They were developing radio-location systems. Sergey held quite a prominent position in the Ministry of Defense. The most prominent brother was Aleksey, chief engineer of the Laboratory of Nuclear Problems, the first Soviet Nuclear Center, in Dubna. The laboratory, under the scientific leadership of Igor Kurchatov, a well-known nuclear physicist, constructed the then (1949) world's largest nuclear accelerator, a proton synchrocyclotron.

Aleksey died young, so I don't remember him, but I remember visiting his wife, Maria. It must have been shortly after her husband's death, because although too young to understand what was happening, I felt the immense sadness emanating from this woman, standing amid a huge expanse of beautiful shiny floors. The rooms were so big that they seemed to me, who was used to much smaller places, to be practically devoid of any furniture. This stark contrast between the sunny beautiful apartment and the sadness of the hostess was precisely what made me remember her and the apartment so vividly. Maria could never accept her husband's untimely death. She did not outlive him by much, leaving two children, a son and a daughter.

Nikolai used to play the guitar and was always tinkering, constructing something. Every flat surface in his apartment was covered with dozens of unfamiliar and intriguing pieces along with plain nuts and bolts. The smell of the solder intertwined with the mouthwatering aroma of freshly baked buns, whisked up and put in the oven almost immediately upon our arrival by his wife Mara. I also liked her wonderful embroideries a great deal. Any skill or talent fascinated me from early on. She was so good, she used to replicate some well-known paintings. We would have tea and chat.

Then, Uncle Kolia, as my father used to call him, would play his guitar. I would not go so far as to say that I am musically challenged, to use the fashionable euphemism instead of the downright unflattering but more to the point *tone-deaf*, but I am certainly not very gifted in this area, as I had stated earlier. I loved to hear him play, nonetheless. I didn't want the music to stop; it seemed to me I could sit there and listen for hours.

Another drawing force of this family was their daughter Eugenia, who was about ten years older than me and whom I adored. She had always been very patient with me and didn't mind entertaining me. She always had a lot of interesting things in stock. I liked her huge cactus the most. It was about a yard high, and a novelty to me. Its tropical silhouette looked incongruous against the backdrop of the window in winter when the windowpanes were covered with beautiful frost designs. Most of our visits were during the cold months, since we spent summers in the country. The thing that fascinated me the most, however, was her hair. It went down to her waist and was usually done in a braid that was probably thicker than my two upper arms put together. My hair was not particularly noteworthy, so she was my idol in that respect.

Truth be told, her cousin, Aleksey's daughter Tatiana, had equally good hair. She was older than Eugenia, however, and existed, as far as I was concerned, in a different realm—that of adults. Alexandra's granddaughter, Elena, had probably the most spectacular hair of them all. Not only was it the thickest, but it was a very beautiful shade of auburn, too. It must have been the shade brave Hastings was so impartial to. I was in awe. Elena was one year older than me, and we had a lot of fun playing together, but the main thing that made me like her so much and single her out among my many friends and relatives was precisely her hair. To this day, I think that the only other woman who could have at least considered competing with her was probably Simonetta Vespucci, the prototype of Sandro Botticelli's Venus.

We had quite a large number of engineers not only on the paternal side, but on the maternal side as well, including my own Uncle Lev, my mother's brother. His desk was piled high with semiconductors of all colors, and the same smell of the soldering gum, one of the favorite smells of my childhood, along with the smell of the car tires on a hot summer day, seemed to have had indelibly permeated the room atmosphere.

He was nineteen when I was born, and our relationship was a rocky one at first. We caused each other a lot of pain occasionally, when I was little, but we did have some of the most wonderful times together afterward.

His girlfriend gave him a little stuffed toy fox for his twenty-second birthday. I hadn't even turned three at the time, and I wanted this cute toy so badly, I used to cry at night. My uncle, being very much in love with that girl at the time, did not cave and would not give it to me. Good for him, I must say. He eventually broke up with the girl, but he has always cherished the little fox. Worn and lackluster, many years later, it still sat proudly on my uncle's bookshelf.

Inadvertently, I had created havoc in his life on a few occasions. The most unpleasant, by far, was when I decided to build a rocket under the dining table in my grandparents' house. It was shortly after Yuri Gagarin's momentous journey into space on April 12, 1961. I guess I decided to join him on his next trip. At last, a decent use for those mesmerizing colorful tubes of all shapes and sizes from my uncle's desk was found! First, I attached a huge chunk of Play-Doh to the inner side of one of the legs of the dining table. My masterpiece was neatly concealed by the tablecloth, so nobody suspected anything. Then, I proceeded to methodically snatch the semiconductors from my uncle's desk and put them in the Play-Doh. Little by little, the engine took shape. My happiness was short-lived, alas.

Perturbed by my frequent disappearances under the table, my grandmother lifted the tablecloth. The day my engine first saw daylight was certainly not the most glorious moment of my life, contrary to my expectations. In fact, it was probably one of the worst. My uncle had to leave the house to avoid killing me on the spot for ruining dozens of his precious components. Everybody else was pretty much aghast, too. I felt really bad. All of a sudden, my brilliant idea lost its luster, and I realized the harm I had done. The worst part of it was there was nothing much I could do. I was not punished, but the shock and incredulity of my relatives that I could do such a thing affected me deeply, and never again did I take his things, or anybody else's, for that matter, without asking first. A couple years later, when I grew up a little, my uncle would make me wonderful portable radios using the same kind of devices I had destroyed.

He was always on the go, with lots of ideas, lots of friends, whom he bossed around mercilessly, and who still adored him, nevertheless. Early morning fishing trips, long journeys into the forest with the obligatory bonfire, potato-baking and making tea in a samovar with pine cones used to boil water will be forever associated with him in my mind. He is the one who taught me how to find a perfect stick for a fishing rod, how to start a fire with one match in a forest dripping wet after the rain, and how to make a toy boat out of a piece of pine bark.

Our most exciting activity, though, was kite-launching during our stays in the country. The kite was made of two crisscrossed, thin narrow planks of plywood and a newspaper glued on top. A long wisp of an old mop was invariably its tail, to my utmost delight. We would wait for an especially windy day and go into the fields, following a narrow earthy path among ears of wheat nodding their heavy heads and whispering something... As the wind picked up, their murmur became louder and louder, as if they were trying to steal our attention devoted solely to the infinite blue sky above. The kite would soar higher and higher. We gazed until our necks became stiff. But what a feeling of triumph!

It was after one such outing that my father chose to tell me the Icarus myth. Whether it just reminded him of the aspiring Greek astronaut or he had sensed I needed a lesson in humility, I will never know. When our daughters were growing up, I "cranked it up a notch," so to say, to steel Emeril Lagasse's favorite expression. I read all the Greek myths to our girls when they were preschoolers. They loved these stories, and because I also encouraged them to draw illustrations to match the myths, we had a lot of images of the Greek gods and heroes lying around our apartment for quite some time. It was my father who was able to track down the particular book on Greek and Roman mythology that I had in mind after seeing it at my friend's house. It was during the pre-Internet age, so he had to visit a dozen bookstores and drive around half of the city to find it. No wonder that when he finally emerged on our doorstep, he was holding the book as if it were a long-lost treasure he had fished from the bottom of the sea.

Since the Icarus talk took place a few years after my own aborted space mission under my grandparents' dining table, I felt it was no wonder that wax did not do the trick. I could just see a small lonely figure with huge white wings high in the limitless sky, the equally immense expanse of the sea beneath. The wax slid along the beautiful white feathers and dripped treacherously down into the sea, its big drops glistening in the sun, as if they were tears.

Along with such books as *The Gadfly, Fountainhead,* and many others, this myth has been to me, ever since, first and foremost, a tale about the tragic beauty and extreme loneliness of a human daring to venture outside the boundaries of the safe corridor between complacency and ambition, to set goals beyond the scope of the accepted, to test the limits of human possibilities. It was a tale about the immortal curiosity of the mortal man. Like stepping stones spaced years apart, they have honed this vision of mine, after the first brief hint in my childhood.

Icarus crashed and burned, but for a few brief moments of his flight, he was able to transcend his human limitations and did get closer to the gods. Is it so wrong to seek perfection? We will always try to reach it and probably never will, as knowledge is as limitless as the universe. But the very futility of the endeavor is what makes man so beautiful, and perhaps just a tinge sad. Hubris is not to try to achieve divine heights. This desire is the driving force of all progress, after all. It is to forget that we are bound to return back to Earth to our fellow human beings. Hubris and arrogance are cold and lifeless. Icarus was so vibrantly, so intensely alive.

I did not know the remarkable words of Golda Meir at that time, "Don't be humble... you're not that great." Just as well, I have always felt I was lucky, but I have never entertained any thoughts about my being special, or even wanting to be for that matter. I always abided by the famous words attributed to Socrates, which I learned and liked when I was thirteen, during one of my Latin lessons: *Scio me nihil scire*—I know that I know nothing.

However, there was one brief episode when I was seven years old. I was listening to a radio program about Sofia Kovalevskaya, a well-known female mathematician. She died when she was 41, and I remember not understanding why it was said she died very young. It seemed to me to be such a long life. Anyway, I also remember very clearly that this was when I thought I absolutely had to be famous. The desire was so acute, my heart skipped a beat. It was the only time in my whole life when the thought had ever entered my mind. I guess my preschool years marked the peak of my ambitions, which ebbed and waned by the time I started school.

Sofia Kovalevskaya can also be blamed for the ruined wallpaper in our apartment. It was mentioned in the same program that the walls of her room were covered, when she was 11 years old, with pages from some mathematical textbook, which became her introduction to calculus. This piece of information really gave me food for thought. As a result, the wallpaper in our apartment did not have a clean spot as high as my arm could reach until I went to school. Needless to say, it was not covered with mathematical formulas, but rather with some of my general assessments of my brother's moral qualities and some childish drawings.

Sofia Kovalevskaya holds a special place in my heart because one of my father's favorite expressions, "Say what you know, do what you must, come what may," was also the motto, as I found out years later, of her paper, "On the Problem of the Rotation of a Solid Body about a Fixed Point."

That would not be the only time I would accidentally come across my father's favorite saying. It felt good to find something he liked, something he thought about and found important enough to pass on to his children. It felt as if I was following in my father's footsteps, finding the clues he left for me to discover. They resembled those shiny white pebbles Little Thumb left along his way.

***

My Aunt Nadejda, my father's younger sister, was a psychiatrist. Her husband, Vladimir, also a psychiatrist, was offered the job of the head of a big psychiatric hospital. The job had its trade-offs. Such hospitals had patients who could present a danger to other people, so it was situated not in Moscow, but on the remote islands of a quaint town on the Volga River.

Nadejda was appointed her husband's deputy. They lived in a beautiful house designated as an historical monument of the seventeenth or eighteenth century adjacent to the main building of the hospital. They had three children, a boy and two younger girls, and a live-in housemaid. None of my other relatives had maids, and I considered it rather extravagant and extremely cool. We kept in touch mostly when my aunt stayed with us during her frequent business trips to Moscow, but once in a while we would also visit the whole family during the summer. My cousin Pavel, named after my grandfather, who was one year younger than me, did not pay much attention to us. He was a very smart boy and was fully immersed in his studies. His sister Olga, on the other hand, who was two years younger than me, was invariably my best friend during those stays. The youngest sister, Natalie, was interested only in my brother, who was her age.

Olga was a very active and industrious girl, and we had a lot of fun together, riding our bikes through the endless linen fields dotted with tiny blue flowers for hours on end, mellow, happy with our lives and ourselves, enjoying our youth, our strength, and our freedom. Once, we became victims of what we considered a huge injustice at the time. A potentially violent patient left the premises of the hospital unattended, and the staff could not locate him for a long time. Olga and I had just left on one of our beloved bike trips. The day was especially nice, and we were gone for many hours. Our bikes were gliding noiselessly along the earth path hard and smooth as a stone on the beach. We got a little lost, having been misled by those very linen fields. Linen flowers close up in the afternoon, and we spent quite some time trying to find the road along the blue flowering fields we took that morning. When we finally came home, I was shocked to see my father, standing absolutely motionless, in front of the house. Even from afar I knew something was really wrong. His face was totally devoid of blood. Never before or after had I seen my father in such a state. We were grounded until the very day of our departure, and had to spend the remaining days in the branches of the huge sour cherry tree in my aunt's orchard, eating sinfully delicious berries and lamenting, somewhat hypocritically, the fate that befell us.

Chapter Eleven

My maternal great-grandmother Ekaterina grew up in a village about seventy miles to the north of Moscow. The morning after she got married and moved into the house of her husband, as was the custom in those days, Alexandra, her mother-in-law, woke her up at four o'clock in the morning and instructed her to sit on a bench outside their house. Alexandra, a widow by that time and a mother of three sons, was a tough woman used to respect and subordination, and ran a tight ship in her house. She did not deem my great-grandmother ready to help her with the house chores right away, but she wanted the young Ekaterina to get used to waking up at the crack of dawn to be ready, when the time came, to replace her with the upkeep of the house. My great-grandmother did not perceive her mother-in-law as a wicked old lady. She knew that this was the only way to survive and prosper in the harsh conditions of rural life, where there was no alternative to hard work from dawn to sunset.

During the First World War, when all the men in the family were fighting, these two women managed to have a new house for the young couple built all by themselves. They could not postpone the construction, because the timber had already been purchased when the war started and had to be used by a specific time in order not to get ruined. Wives were allowed to visit their husbands on the front line, and Ekaterina visited her husband Andrey, one of the handsomest men in the village, and relayed all the news to him. The house withstood both World Wars, and was considered one of the best in her village even many years later. When foreign delegations came to visit the village's collective farm, her house was usually shown as a model of a typical Soviet rural household.

Ekaterina's mother came from an affluent family. She had two brothers who had a very successful business; they owned the village restaurant. They did not approve of their sister's choice of a husband, who was as poor as a church mouse. Apparently, it did not affect her much, since it was common knowledge that she and her daughters (Ekaterina had three sisters and two brothers) were among the cheeriest people in the whole village, their laughter being heard late into the evening hours, as all of the villagers could attest.

Grandma Katia, as my mother used to call her, learned all the tricks of the trade, and although she had lost her husband rather early due to an accident—he was kicked by a horse in the abdomen area and died shortly after—she had a solid, comfortable life. She worked all her life. Her favorite saying has always been that "manna does not fall from the sky." I don't think she ever owned a TV, but she read the Bible every night.

Quietly religious herself, she never tried to proselytize her beliefs, but nevertheless had her grandchildren baptized the moment they wound up in her custody. She did not dream of hiding her intentions, but she certainly did not advertise them either, so that her atheist son and his wife, both 22 when my mother was born, had to deal with a fait accompli.

I'm sure she did it quite serenely, without experiencing any feelings of guilt or even a shade of discomfort. That is not to say she did not understand or was not ready to acknowledge the new rules of the game and even to use them to her advantage. Shortly after the war the need to install some military personnel in her village arose during reconstruction work by German prisoners. The commander was going door-to-door looking for volunteers to put up some soldiers for a few weeks. She told him she would be delighted to, but her grandchildren were staying with her at the time. "The children of a diplomat," she added pointedly.

Glancing at two kids who looked more like children from a foreign trophy movie than from the local village, the man felt no need to go into the matter any further. "In that case, sorry to have bothered you," he said, saluting her on his way out.

She could read and weave lace without glasses until late into her seventies, as her mother-in-law used to do. Her bed had always had an elaborate lace skirt and a huge pile of pillows of different sizes, with lace covers. She had a huge trunk with her dowry, still in perfect shape, that she used to show my mother. Dresses, woolen skirts to go to church, shawls. She bought them herself, while still a young girl, when she went to work in St. Petersburg for a few months with precisely this goal in mind. Even later in life, she never let her younger counterparts outdo her. Once, already after the war, she noticed the new fancy underskirts of some younger women. Ekaterina did not go to bed that night, but the next morning she came to work wearing a breezy concoction of frills and lace, peeping discreetly out from under her usual long work skirt from time to time.

Ekaterina had two children, two sons, who lived to adulthood. My grandfather's younger brother was killed early during the war. She lost two boys in their early childhood to scarlet fever and her baby daughter Ksenia to diphtheria. She breast-fed and raised as her own the daughter of her husband's younger brother, Vassily. He and his wife, who had just given birth, died from the Spanish flu the same day as Ksenia.

When German troops occupied her village and the entire population hid in the nearby woods after having buried all their most precious belongings, she used to surreptitiously come every morning to her house to fire up her oven. She was scared the German soldiers would burn the house if they did it themselves, her love for her house overriding her fear of losing her life. The occupation did not last longer than a few days, but the Russian troops lost a lot of men during this brief period, trying to regain the village. A German soldier with a machine-gun hid on top of the church's belfry. The church stood amid the village fields, and the Russian soldiers who were trying to reach it had nowhere to hide. When they finally managed to get to him and regain control over the village, the earth around the belfry was littered with hundreds of dead and wounded men.

My great-grandmother and her fellow villagers considered themselves lucky, however. Thousands of villages were wiped off of the face of the earth during the war, their occupants killed or shipped off to concentration camps. No SS battalions, especially notorious for their cruelty toward the civilian population, were stationed in their village, and there were no punitive operations. They learned later that the SS troops stopped just six miles away.

When Ekaterina became a widow, her sister Anna came from the city to live with her. Anna never married, did not mind a little vodka once in a while, and smoked unfiltered cigarettes all her life. One image of her became stuck in my memory—her long skirts tucked high to avoid dirtying them in the mud after the rain, her blue eyes shining with determination and her eternal cigarette glued to her lips, an ax in one hand and a chicken in the other, getting ready to celebrate our arrival with fresh chicken soup.

Ekaterina and Anna both lived well into their nineties and the family consensus was that they would have lived even longer were it not for a fire that consumed their house and proved a very painful blow to both sisters. I remember celebrating New Year's Eve at our place, and my father wishing her, 86 at that time, to live until 100, and my intense desire for that wish to come true. She lived to be 96. Her sister died in the subway, at about the same age, while running her daily errands. Grandmother Katia was very smart in her quiet demure ways. As long as she lived, while growing up, I remember hearing other relatives, whenever they needed a few rubles to last until the next salary or a more substantial amount of money, to say the same thing, over and over: "We should ask Grandmother Katia."

When Ekaterina finally retired, my grandfather took her sickle, the tool she was so handy with, and displayed it on a wall in the living room of his country house. It happened to be the wall on which the icons should have been hung, had he been a religious man. That was only too appropriate. Ekaterina had lived all her life by God and by sickle.

***

My grandfather, Ilya, her oldest son, was born in a rather matter-of-fact fashion in 1912, five years before the revolution. "Where are you going, Katia?" asked her neighbor. "I'm going to give birth," she replied. A couple of hours later, when she was going home with a small bundle, the neighbor asked her the same question. "I'm going home with the baby," she replied.

Until his younger brother was born, Ilya was the only boy on the maternal side of his family and was spoiled by his mother's rich uncles, who used to give him rides in their horse carriage and feed him in their restaurant. When he was about two or three years old, he would try to sneak out some jam in his mouth for his outcast grandfather. He was the only member of our family who preferred opera to drama. He would spend hours in the church singing in the choir.

He married my grandmother, Olga, when they were both twenty years old. He had a room in the dormitory of the chemistry institute he was studying at and she had a studio apartment. They chose to live in the studio apartment. After the civil war, there was a huge shortage of residential buildings in Moscow, and a studio was considered a luxury. Most people lived in communal apartments, where a few families shared one big place, with one room per family and shared kitchen and bathroom. Many families lived in cellars.

By the time my mother was born, a couple of years later, things got worse. The building was an old two-story one. The pipes leaked and one corner of the room was always damp. My mother was sick all the time. Finally, in the middle of winter, when it was usually around minus 30 degrees Celsius outside, the doctor who was attending her, exasperated, told Olga, "Dear mamma, take the baby, dress her as warmly as you can and go outside. Do so every day and stay outside as long as you can." It worked.

There was no gas stove in their apartment, as was usually the case with old townhouses, and people used portable stoves on kerosene to prepare food. I still remember them; we used one in our summer rental house when I was a preschooler. The kerosene store was just outside the house, and to buy it, Olga tried to sneak out while the baby was sleeping. She was so scared the baby would wake up, she kept returning to check on her dozens of times before she could muster enough courage to dart to the store. She could not handle a baby and the kerosene container at the same time. She really needed two free hands to haul it upstairs to the second floor.

When my mother was two, she came down with scarlet fever and needed hospitalization. The same old doctor told Olga that in Moscow mothers were not allowed to stay in hospitals with children older than two, but that it was possible in the surrounding towns. "Do you have any relatives outside the capital, anybody at all?" he asked her. Olga grabbed my mother and went to her mother-in-law, Ekaterina. She stayed in the hospital with my mother for more than a month. When my grandfather came to take them home, my mother was very intrigued by some strange but beautiful round objects he had in his bag that she had never seen before. They were oranges. It was 1936. The war in Spain had started.

This proved to be the last straw. My grandparents found a new place to live. They did not have enough money to exchange their studio for a better one, so they had to take a room in a communal apartment. It was a corner room, however, with two huge windows and plenty of light, dry and warm. They shared this apartment with two or three other families. They also shared one telephone number, and the phone hung in the hall. Whoever was closest would pick up and fetch the person the call was intended for. The procedure was different as far as visitors were concerned. A special little code was in place. Every family was assigned a certain number of rings, and guests were supposed to ring the appropriate amount of times. My grandparents got the number three. For many years, long after they had gotten their own apartment, their friends and relatives would continue to ring three times, whenever they came to visit. To this day, I always ring three times, no matter where I go, as a little secret wink to my grandparents.

When my mother got a little older, Olga thought it was time to go back to work. She was an aviation mechanic by training. Her familiarity with the aviation engine, however, could not help her now. She had greatly enjoyed working at the airports and construction bureau before she became a mother, but now she needed something tamer and closer to home. She had always loved Russian literature. She had often told me that journalism was a wonderful profession. She advised me strongly to consider it. That was probably her own secret dream all along. She wrote great papers when she was in school, and her teachers tried to persuade her to continue her studies in that field.

The village she was living in with her parents had only an elementary school, and older kids had to travel three miles each way to a bigger village, which had a secondary school. By some serendipitous circumstance, it had many teachers with qualifications far exceeding the standard requirements. The fact that people with Moscow University degrees had to become secondary degree teachers in some provincial village was in itself not an unusual occurrence. It was very much in accordance with the zeitgeist, as her own father's story would attest, but such a large number of brilliant scholars teaching at one particular school was, indeed, rare. Her sister, who was seven years younger, always complained that she learned to read in school on very politically correct poems, many of which were of dubious literary merit.

One way or the other, Olga did have a very special and strong affinity for books all her life. She found a great spot at a local library and was very excited to start her new job. Her new career lasted exactly one day. My mother, three at the time, was apparently not very much enthused by the prospect of whiling away her days at a daycare center. She left the premises and walked home. It was more than just a few blocks away, and she had to cross some very busy streets. My grandmother got so terrified that she quit the next day.

In my grandparents' youth, white canvas shoes, which young women used to polish with tooth powder, were all the rage in Moscow. My grandfather bought a pair for my grandmother, too. In order to be able to afford them, he sold his most prized possession—a silver cigarette case. I have always considered this story to be our family's very own version of "The Gift of the Magi." The numerous sparkles of his love landed on me, too. When I was four and he was working in India, he bought me an amazingly beautiful and expensive silk dress. I was his only grandchild at the time. His coworkers were telling him, "You are crazy, Ilya." It was not possible to buy such dresses in Moscow at that time, and I felt like a little princess.

Maybe it is not a coincidence that it was my grandmother who introduced me to the O. Henry original in the first place. In her turn, my grandmother had a clean shirt, an ironed suit, and hot breakfast for him ready in the morning, and dinner waiting for him in the evening, never skipping a day in all of their fifty-plus years together. Even today it would require some planning, if not much work. In the Russia of the first half of the twentieth century, it was hard manual work, aggravated even further by the fact that after the war, soap was one of the already mentioned rationed products. Needless to say, the laundry detergent was nonexistent.

Before washing machines became available, shirts, as everything else, including bed linens, had to be washed in a basin. Irons in those years were chunky cast-iron affairs that left no question as to where the name "iron" came from. The iron had to be heated on the stove and heated just right, not to burn the fabric. Another long-lost skill of those times was to fill your mouth full of water and sprinkle it evenly on the fabric before ironing it in order to evenly moisten it. Irons not only lacked temperature dials, they did not come with any vapor settings, either. My grandmother mastered this skill to perfection, and I remember trying in vain to emulate her during every such ironing session. Where she acquired the patience to deal with endless soggy pieces of clothing after my unsuccessful experiments is beyond me. Words like, "Not now, I'm busy" or "Don't touch, you're too young," were not in her vocabulary. Everything was fun with her—doing laundry in a huge basin with a washboard, ironing clothes, dragging carpets outside to clean them in the first snow, getting a piece of meat from behind the window in the wintertime, where it was hanging to avoid getting spoiled in the absence of refrigerators. I was watching her strong dexterous hands and wanted to copy her, although I never really loved or expressed any deep interest in domestic activities, per se.

My grandmother had a sewing machine, a beautiful foot-operated Zinger device. Considering the scarcity of clothes for sale in Moscow stores at that time, it was an indispensable and cherished item. She did not particularly like sewing, however, and had always had a seamstress, which was what many women did in those years. The only time I saw this machine working for hours on end was when my brother was about to be born. Those were the dark pre-Pampers ages, and one could not have enough cloth diapers. Scores of my grandfather's and my uncle's old shirts and any pieces of fabric big enough to serve the purpose were mercilessly cut to size and hemmed by my tireless grandmother. Anyway, I was allowed to try the machine, and I mastered the basic forward stitch pretty decently.

My grandfather Ilya left the running of the house entirely to my grandmother. Since the day he married her and up until his death, he would leave his salary and ultimately his pension in the cupboard drawer in the living room. He put his foot down only twice in family matters—once for my mom not to lose one year, the fourth grade, when she had to change schools, and once for her to go back to school and get her master's degree after I was born.

He bought his first car when he was in his fifties and learned to drive shortly thereafter, undeterred by the young age of the fellow students at the driving school. My grandparents had built a country house by that time, and I remember his serious and concentrated face, at the wheel of his new car, taking us all to visit.

He continued working various odd jobs after he retired, although he was not a very healthy man at that time. Once, when my parents were in Switzerland with my brother and I was living alone, he happened to be working not far from where we lived. He stopped by, bringing me steaks, to feed me. He was in his mid-sixties. I was twenty.

My maternal grandmother Olga was the oldest child of a self-made man on the rise. As luck would have it, he had bought a country house just months before the revolution took place. It was a beautiful house on a large plot of land with a small forest, in a picturesque area to the south of the capital.

The new state of workers and peasants abolished private property and nationalized the main means of production, notably, the land. My great-grandfather Piotr was told by the authorities that he had to choose between his Moscow apartment and the newly acquired country house. He could not keep both and was not able to sell, either, as he was no longer considered the owner. He also had to let go of the forest. Many people with means fled the country at that point, leaving behind most of their belongings. Many houses just stood empty, abandoned by their owners.

My great-grandfather was so fond of his new big, beautiful house! He spent so much time finding it, and so much time saving for it. He was not ready to give it up, not just yet, not right away. He chose the house. Besides, he thought it would be easier to feed his growing family in the country during those hungry times of civil unrest.

In a few weeks, if not days, my great-grandparents and their two young children (my grandmother was six at that time) left Moscow to start a new life they knew nothing about. The freshly minted proletarians were given a separate train carriage, a great luxury at the time, to help them with the move. The order was signed by Lenin himself.

It proved to be a choice full of hardships. City dwellers through and through, my great-grandparents had no knowledge of the country life and had trouble adjusting to it in the beginning. The rural community did not accept them readily, as was to be expected, and offered them no preferential treatment. On the contrary, as newcomers, they got the worst land plot to work on, and in general, were treated with caution and mistrust. The beautiful furniture brought from Moscow mostly landed in the attic and was sold piece by piece, to help feed the family, but the marble bathroom basins and shiny brass faucets stayed, as did the garden, where my great grandfather would plant specimens from various nurseries so successfully, his garden would become well known in the area.

***

Relegated back to square one, Piotr was faced with the necessity of rebuilding his life from scratch. He became a schoolteacher. Marfa, his wife, took care of the family. After a while, my great-grandfather succeeded in earning love and respect in his village, and my grandmother would hear reverential whispers behind her back wherever she went, "Look, look, here comes the teacher's daughter!" My grandmother enjoyed Easter the most, when her father would don his Moscow attire complete with his cane and they would all go to church.

My grandmother contributed her small share to the family's toils, too. Her mother would send her to the forest at sunrise to pick mushrooms. Then Marfa would quickly boil them and sell them to passengers of the passing train that used to stop at their station for a few minutes. My grandmother would run as fast as she could and yell at the top of her lungs. The dew was icy cold, and my grandmother was barefoot. There was a shortage of shoes in the country.

When my grandmother turned 18, disaster hit. At that time, she was already studying in Moscow and lived with her maternal grandmother. She was coming home one day, walking up the stairs to her apartment. As she was approaching her floor, her footsteps became slower and slower, until she finally stopped at her door, unable to force herself to ring the bell. She did not know how long she remained there, but suddenly the front door opened and she saw her grandmother, holding a letter in her hands, crying. My grandmother said just one word, "Mother?" and her grandmother replied, "Yes."

My great-grandmother died at the age of 44 in childbirth. She left six children; the youngest one, Boris, was three years old. Piotr never remarried and raised his children alone. Olga remained in Moscow and continued her studies.

These children felt their loss very deeply. Once, her brother, himself already a man of forty-odd and a father of three, called her to say hello upon returning from an overseas trip. He said he didn't call earlier because his wife had been on the phone with her mother for almost an hour and the line was busy. "She is so lucky, Olga," he said. "She has a mother."

Olga's father, though not a wealthy man anymore, would regularly send her money to go to the theater, in an attempt to distract and cheer her up a little. She was the biggest drama fan in our family. It was with her that I went to the theater for the first time, to see my first play. It was a play by a well-known Russian playwright, Alexander Ostrovsky, *Enough Stupidity in Every Wise Man*, in the famous Moscow Art Theatre named after Maxim Gorky. This has always been one of the most beloved theaters in Moscow, although there were many great theaters in the capital at that time. Dramatic art, together with opera and ballet, has historically been extremely popular in Russia. The repertoires of the theaters were monitored closely, and tickets to the best performances sold out very quickly. These modern temples of Melpomene were treated as such. The true aficionados would not dream of wearing jeans to a performance, and women always changed their winter boots for dress shoes once inside.

Still, the play would most probably have been lost on me, just a preteen at that time, if it weren't for my grandmother. She made me see what could almost have been a school project for what it really was, that is, a great work of art. She knew the play practically by heart, as well as all the actors, which were indeed a wonderful bunch. Her enthusiasm was so genuine, so devoid of any pretense or affectation, she made me learn to love them, too.

The physical burden of their mother's death fell on Olga's only sister, Anastasia. She was thirteen when their mother died, and still living with her parents. Once, at some family reunion, she suddenly burst into tears, remembering how she had to take care of the family and take over practically all of her mother's tasks. One of her chores was to fetch water from the well for the entire family, two huge buckets at a time. She would plunge the bucket down into the well, and would have no strength to pull it up when it was full. She would just stay there, pulling at the rope and crying, until some sympathetic woman would come to the well and rescue her from her predicament. I was listening and looking at her, a successful pediatrician; at her thin beautiful face, her smart clothes, and her knotty hands, too big for her frail frame, clasping a handkerchief.

The train of our lives runs busily along its seemingly predictable course. The passengers go peacefully about their business or sleep serenely in their berths, unsuspicious of any imminent route changes. At some junctions, though, unbeknownst to the travelers, the train is bound to change its direction. It could be just a slight turn, an imperceptible course adjustment, but it could also prove to be a major unforeseen change of the anticipated itinerary. As if some invisible hand had operated the switch on a whim, and when you look back at your tracks after a while, you realize that your journey underwent a momentous deviation at that point, which had significantly influenced your future.

Chapter Twelve

In October of 1940, my grandfather was offered an assignment in Sweden. My grandparents, along with their two children, my mother, six at the time, and her baby brother Lev, bordered a red-colored Scandinavian plane and left the country less than a year before Hitler attacked the Soviet Union for one of the few European countries which remained neutral during World War II. The family would spend more than four years in an oasis of relative security and abundance amid the raging fires of destruction and death.

When the war began, my grandfather hung a huge map on the living room wall and would mark the position of the Russian troops with red flags, which my mother would help him move as the troops advanced or retreated. That was the time she would learn to read. Her ABCs were the daily information sheets of the Soviet Information Bureau about the situation on the fronts.

For many long months the family watched the flags get closer and closer to Moscow. My grandfather was very worried about his mother when he recognized the village only a few miles away from the one he was born in, and where his mother still lived in a photo in a newspaper. The village was closer to Moscow than hers, and it was clear that it was under German occupation. That meant that her village was probably occupied, too. There was no way to get in touch with any of his relatives, however.

Postal communication with the Soviet Union resumed through diplomatic channels only about a year into the war. Upon returning from school, my mother found her mother in tears over a letter. She had never seen her mother cry before. That in itself was a great shock to her. This was the first letter after a long period of silence without any news from home. It was not a happy one. Her younger brother Victor was killed a few months after the war had started. He was 18 years old.

Time passed. The red flags on the map were slowly moving west, the iron grip of the enemy was weakening, the beast was dying. Victory was still far off, but at least it was a matter of time. The feelings of uncertainty and anxiety gave way to a more cheerful, more optimistic atmosphere.

Toward the end of the war, Olga started taking her children to the local movie theaters. American movies were very popular. They especially enjoyed *Tarzan* and the Disney movies. *Bambi* was my mother's favorite. There were also occasional outings to a local cafe. Olga would treat her daughter (her son being too young to appreciate such decadent items) to a large cup of coffee and a rolled cream-stuffed pastry. Olga never bought anything for herself, and just enjoyed the delight in her little girl's eyes while inhaling the wonderful aroma of freshly brewed coffee. Many years later, having traveled all over the world with her husband, having dined in many of the world's best restaurants and attended many high-level receptions, my mother would still speak about this experience with the same unfailing awe. This is the only gustatory experience my mother would mention time and time again. Were she to be invited to Buckingham Palace to High Tea with the Queen of England, she would probably not be as thrilled as she was to sip her coffee and look into her mother's smiling face.

***

In March of 1945, the family could finally go home. They were traveling by rail, changing trains in Leningrad. The city had withstood a 900-day blockade. The siege had been lifted more than a year before, and the city was just beginning to come back to normal life again. The train for Moscow was not leaving until the next day. A car was waiting at the railway station to take the family to their hotel. The ride took no more than ten minutes. The car was moving slowly along the streets of hollowed buildings that often had only some parts of their facades still intact, with shadowy people moving noiselessly along them. The once elegant and brilliant imperial capital now resembled the sinister grin of an old pauper with just a few black, decaying teeth left. Not a single glass pane to reflect the cheerful spring rays in sight, not a single curtain to protect from prying eyes. And what use would curtains be, anyway, when very often all one could see through the empty window frames was the sky?

It was a brutal crash course in what their country had gone through.

This was the true face of war. Piping-hot cocoa and oatmeal with mountain cranberries for breakfast and huge green soap bars filling the bathroom with aromas of fresh meadow became, in one short instant, irretrievably distant and irrelevant. The chocolate bar in my mother's purse felt heavy, awkward, incongruous.

In Moscow, Anastasia, whom my grandmother had not seen since the beginning of the war, met them at the railway station. She was a yellowish wisp of a human being with two thin pigtails instead of the healthy plump girl with red cheeks, a ready smile and a head full of hair, crying while mourning the death of her father earlier that year.

She had just come back from the evacuation to Omsk, a city in Siberia, where she had been sent with her medical school when staying in Moscow became too dangerous, and where she was studying for her exams with rats, emboldened by hunger, keeping her company.

After the war, the rules were very strict as far as people coming to visit the capital. The visitors were not allowed to stay with their Moscow relatives or friends for long periods of time. My grandparents had to disregard this rule, however, on many occasions. Olga, being the oldest sister, assumed the moral responsibility for her siblings. Throughout her life, and she died two weeks before her ninetieth birthday, she never lost sight of them, and helped them whenever and however she could.

Olga's brother, Anatoly, still in the army but enrolled in law school, lived with them when studying for his exams. The other, older brother, Leonid, who fought on the Far East front and served there for a few years after the war was over, stayed with them, too, whenever he came to visit. He was the only professional military man in our family. It took him two weeks to get to Moscow—only train transportation was available then—and another two weeks to get back. He came just for a few days, which was all that was left of his one month-long vacation, to briefly see his brothers and sisters before going back.

Once, shortly after the end of the war, when food rationing was still in place, he wrote to Olga that he was coming to visit. He was still single, and Olga, knowing that officers got very good food supplies before their vacation, was hoping he would bring some food to supplement their modest rations. She was astonished when he came home empty-handed. It turned out that he had given away all the supplies to his subalterns from other cities, which were worse off than Moscow, the capital. "The newspapers were reporting that Moscow had plenty of food," he said. Everybody laughed for many years at this instance of wishful naïveté on the part of a seasoned military officer.

Every week or so, a militiaman in charge of supervising the district would come to check every apartment for unregistered dwellers. Everybody knew that some unregistered soul was living with my grandparents. The militiaman would stay for a while, have tea with my grandmother, then sigh and just say, "Okay, Anatoly, or Leonid, or Boris, get out from under the table, I know you are hiding there." They never evicted them.

I remember walking with Olga once when I was still a little girl of seven or eight, at most. She kept saying to me, "Suppose you see a wallet in the street. Don't take it. It's not yours. It is not yours." I remember thinking that maybe that was a little excessive, however, I didn't say anything. My grandmother Olga was a great narrator, and probably my first educator in the broad sense of the word. She told me countless stories from books she had read and scores of anecdotes from her own life. The reason my memory singled out this one in particular is because the tone of her voice for an otherwise very calm and poised woman had some ring of uncharacteristic urgency to it. It was somehow out of character and struck a discordant note. As I found out later, even 10 or 12 year-old children, during the hungry postwar years, could go to prison for stealing as little as a handful of peas from a state field. Be that as it may, when more than thirty years after this homily, I did find a wallet on the store floor of a Duane Reade pharmacy in New York City, I brought it to the cashier who looked at me as though I was insane.

Now I think that maybe she was not only trying to teach me the basic difference between right and wrong, but that maybe it was part of her formula for survival itself. On the other hand, come to think of it, does not the ratio of right and wrong in our soul determine, precisely, our personal formula of survival? Whatever it was, her personal integrity was quite remarkable. During the war, some museum collections were hidden from bombings under Moscow bridges. They were still lying there for some time, after the war was over, practically in plain sight, unguarded. She never took anything. She was well-known and respected for her honesty. One episode I heard about her struck me the most. It was shortly after the war, and there were considerable shortages of food. Olga was in the store when suddenly commotion erupted. Meat was brought in unexpectedly. She had no extra money on her. The salesperson, who had worked in the store for a long time and knew all of her regular customers, gave her the meat anyway, trusting her to pay for it the next day.

The only time I ever got annoyed with my grandmother was when I was already in my twenties. I had just gotten married. My in-laws had a big apartment, and again, she was telling me, "It's not yours, don't even think about it. It's not yours." I almost got mad at her, not for telling me this, but for thinking I needed to be told.

My grandmother was a very strong woman. When typhus, which was a scourge for the first few years after the revolution, was raging all over the country, she was the only one in her family who did not contract it, even though all of her siblings and both her parents had it and she remained in direct contact with them. Twenty-five million Russians came down with the disease during those years and over 2.5 million died from it.

She was not just physically strong. She possessed that rare gift of good-humored generous spiritual strength that drew people to her, like a magnet. Everybody came to her both in happy times or in times of need, it happened quite naturally. Everybody always felt genuinely welcomed by her, and very much at ease.

I never saw her complain, I never saw her flinch. She just put on her heels.

Of all my relatives, besides my parents, I spent the most time with my grandmother. In the forty-four years that I knew her, I never discovered the limits of her soul. She was larger than life, very smart, and very generous. What was her secret? She used the Golden Rule. It was an integral part of who she was. It was as simple and as complicated as that. The rules are sometimes so simple to understand, but so very hard to follow.

She liked people. She never pushed anybody away, never judged, never asked for anything in return. She would chat people up in trains, in store queues, in doctors' waiting rooms. She knew how to listen to them. She also knew how to talk. Her command of the Russian language, the only language she knew, was superb. Even as a very young child I loved to listen to her talk. She was the epicenter: her big family, numerous friends and acquaintances revolved around her, and I was there in tow, taking it all in, observing life itself with all of its dramas, big and small, unfurling in front of my very eyes. I was a spectator, getting a free preview.

As in photography, where a short time after the sunrise and before the sunset, often referred to as the "golden hours" for the best lighting conditions, the ideal time to observe life is probably in childhood and in old age. We have the sharpest instincts in nonage and the greatest experience in advanced years. One gets the truest picture precisely because this is the time of contemplation rather than that of action. As Jackie Robinson put it, "Life is not a spectator sport."

***

The twentieth century was a difficult one in world history, and Russia was by no means spared. When I was born, the turmoil and devastation of the 1917 Russian Revolution, of the ensuing Civil War, and of the Great Patriotic War were already banished from the land, but in human minds, the scars remained. The earth is so much more resilient than human memory. Grass will grow and flowers will bloom where once bombs ripped open the soil and dead human bodies were piled one on top of the other for as long as the eye could see. But a child will always remember his lost father, and a mother will never forget her lost son. The wound never really heals, the soul just burns until there seems to be nothing left to burn anymore, and nothing left anymore to hurt, and only a numb emptiness remains.

But it seems those were not the only marks these wars have left on the living. After the nightmare was over, grief, despair, memories of the atrocities notwithstanding, there seemed to be a very powerful urge to just live and be happy, and probably to remain human, no matter what. Being born just thirteen years after the end of World War II, I must have caught the waning years of this truly rapturous pleasure of just being alive, before people settled into their familiar daily routine and started wondering what color their next couch was going to be.

Chapter Thirteen

I made it a nighttime activity to read to the girls. We kept this tradition until they left for college. They loved this time since they were toddlers, especially because it would postpone the time I would turn off the light and ask them to go to sleep. Two pairs of attentive eyes, round with curiosity, would look at me from atop the bed covers, taking in every word. They would not move and I would bet they tried occasionally to hold their breath. It was such a delight to see how one emotion replaced the other, until the stare became less focused and the eyelids trembled in a desperate effort to keep the eyes from closing. These reading sessions would sometimes last for almost an hour, and after a while I would begin to look for these signals with tired impatience. I would hastily wrap up the story and sneak out of the room at their very onset.

When the girls got a little older and the novels such as *The Three Musketeers, The Headless Horseman, The Gadfly,* and many others substituted the children's books, I would be as enthralled as they were. Pretty often, we would stay up way past their bedtime as I would read for hours on end. Although I was familiar with most of them, I got even more pleasure from introducing these great books to the girls than from reading them myself in my childhood. On top of that, I was witnessing the same phenomenon time and time again. One is never done with a great book. It is like an onion. Every time you read it, you take off a few additional layers, realize that there was so much you did not pick up on the previous time, and chances are there would be more facets to discover when you reread it in a few years. You never outgrow it.

To expose those endless facets of life without passing judgment requires a great talent. Otherwise, your work will not, in all likelihood, withstand the test of time, for ideas come and go, and your interpretation may become obsolete over time and present, at best, only an historical interest. A great book teaches you to think and come to your own conclusions. But this was very much what I wanted to do as a parent, and I realized our education method should be akin to such a great book. We should not instill ready solutions, for they limit the amount of problems our child can solve to the familiar, and who knows what life has in store for our child? He or she has to be able to adopt to the changing reality, to possess some kind of universal key to tackle life's problems. Many years later I read that critical thinking skills trump simple rote memorization in our increasingly fast-paced and diversified economy. Indeed, "drop everything and read," as the girls' school slogan went.

Of course, my love for global reach and absolute coverage of material did not fail to manifest itself. For starters, I checked "The Great Books of the Western World" collection of the Encyclopedia Brittanica that we had acquired by that time. I would also ferret out lists of books, be it "100 Books to Read in your Lifetime," or "The Best Books of the Millennium," or "200 Books Everyone Should Read," not to mention lists of books recommended for summer reading. For some time, I did manage to keep pretty close to the lists and also to read every book our girls read myself, in an attempt to be able to see the world with their eyes.

As counterintuitive as it seemed, my regular out-loud readings to our children did not prevent them from starting to read on their own. It was akin to an explosion, and I just could not keep up with them anymore. I had to let go. It did not come easy. For a long time, it felt like I was left behind, looking at the fast, beautiful caravel disappearing on the horizon. But we must let go when the time comes. This is a huge unfairness of life, in my view, that the more we love our children, the more we suffer, because it is so much harder to let go of them, and yet we have to do it, proper child-raising techniques be damned.

Children react differently when exposed to the same stimuli. Why upon hearing a piece of news about some successful hacker's security breach would one person rush to his computer to devise a better hacker program while some other guy would work on a better security scheme, with dozens of options in between?

Siblings are exposed to a similar routine and go through the same process, yet the results are usually very different. So, following this thought to its logical conclusion, parents probably should treat siblings differently to obtain similar results. And we usually do treat them differently, sometimes without realizing it.

From the very beginning, our girls were very different, even in small funny ways. As a toddler, Lydia was addicted to the bottle, be it milk, juice, or water. She would run around the playground, and her bottle seemed permanently glued to the corner of her mouth, like Popeye's pipe. Nathalie, on the other hand, never took anything with a rubber nipple in her mouth and drank from a training cup when the time came to introduce liquids other than breast milk. Maybe this is not the best example of the girls' differences, come to think of it, because it probably has a lot to do with the fact that I stopped giving Nathalie a pacifier after she was only a few months old. I don't remember whether I heard it on the news or through the mothers' grapevine, but there seemed to be a recall on some brand of pacifiers. I got so scared, I decided not to take chances with any of them, and literally just snatched it from Nathalie's mouth. She did not seem to mind.

Lydia liked Cream of Wheat with raspberries or blueberries for breakfast while Nathalie preferred oatmeal with strawberries. During our frequent car trips, Lydia would ask for Chicken McNuggets, while Nathalie preferred Chicken Tenders from Burger King. I would cook two breakfasts and we would find rest areas with both restaurants, all the while sighing under our breath, Alex and I, for he was hoping for a Kentucky Fried Chicken and I liked Taco Bell.

Of course, I myself was hardly the same person when Lydia and Nathalie were born. I traveled a long way from the frightened, inexperienced novice to a secure and confident mother. When Lydia started crawling, I would run after her, putting clean sheets on the sofa in front of her. When Nathalie started crawling, she did so on the playground, and I did not mind a bit.

We are so easily fooled by the monikers we attribute to things and people! As long as the name is the same, we assume it is the same person or the same thing. Quite often it is very far from the truth. I dubbed it the "Brie Syndrome." At the very onset of our married life, Alex and I got carried away once and bought a wheel of Brie cheese on sale at a fraction of its original cost. The cheese had a brownish moist crust and it pretty much stunk up everything in our fridge. Whatever the name of that thing was, it was not Brie.

I did not try to teach Lydia to read until she was almost five. Being the unchallenged older child, she was in no hurry. Lydia learned the letters and mastered the process very fast, but was not at all interested in reading herself. I tried many different approaches. I tried to cajole her and to outright bribe her. I would give her books with great colorful illustrations. I put a children's armchair in the girls' room and called it the "reading chair" to make reading look like a special treat. Lydia remained unconvinced and unenthused until one day when I took her with me to my doctor's appointment. There was another child in the waiting room with his mother, a boy about her age. He was whiling away the time by reading out loud from all the medical posters on the walls. It was very clear that Lydia was impressed. Almost immediately after we came home that day, she picked up a book and started reading.

Nathalie learned letters when she was three and was reading fluently by three and a half. It was Nathalie who would bring me the wooden letters, and later a book, the first chance she got, and ask me to teach her. I was not at all surprised. Nathalie had been trying to keep up with the older crowd since she was a baby. Once, when she was barely one year old, I put her into her crib and went out to check on something in the kitchen. When I was back, I found my daughter balancing on the crib rail, holding my mascara, which was lying on a high dresser close to the crib, and all but poking it into her eye. How she got on the rail, got hold of the mascara, and managed to open it remains a mystery.

***

I never entertained any thoughts of artistic or musical careers for the girls. Children of artists and musicians are usually assumed to have inherited the talent from their parents and are expected to follow in their footsteps. In that respect, our girls were free as birds. Both Alex and I had no relatives in those circles, and I had no reason to expect any particular abilities from them. The burden of proof would be on our children. Still, when Lydia was five, I began to look for appropriate venues for her to take lessons. Nathalie would join as soon as I could sneak in a younger sibling.

At some point, I learned about an art group for very young kids. The teacher was the former head of an art school for children. Being well over seventy, she had been retired for many years already by that time. She was a real enthusiast. She looked very frail and delicate, but she still had a lot of authority and spunk. Parents, most from the art world, were trying to help their kids to make their work better almost before the children started painting, and were whispering their advice to their progeny at every opportunity. Standing in a close circle around the easels, they looked very much like a pack of hungry wolves about to jump in and snatch the brushes from their child's hands. The teacher would get extremely angry, and I could see that at times she was very tempted to use her pointing stick to chase us away.

She kept repeating that parents should be patient, that it is of paramount importance that children form their own vision independently and learn to find their own ways to translate this vision into a painting or any other work of art. They should not be rushed or, worse, influenced at this point. As much as parents were usually a source of disappointment and frustration for her, children seemed to be one of delight. She had a way with kids. She was their guide into the art world, showing them renowned masterpieces and explaining to them different techniques artists used to achieve particular effects. She would lead, and they followed her as though she were the Pied Piper. She knew her tune, but mostly, she knew how to see. The canvases spoke to her.

She knew what to make of some random color blotches or some mysterious entanglement of lines. She was always alert, always on the lookout for talent. Fast as a lightning bolt and sharp as a needle, she would grab the loose end of talent the moment it lurked out of the colored mess and would drag it tenaciously into the daylight, for everyone to see and admire. She obviously knew all the telltale signs. Everybody adored her. I still keep a few of the girls' paintings from those classes. One of my favorites is Lydia's lilies of the valley.

The girls' artistic education was not limited to classes. Colored pencils, crayons, and paint were their favorite items in our household. Once, I was able to spot the creative process from the very beginning. When Nathalie was two years old, we went to a park one afternoon and saw hundreds of birds, frightened by someone or something flying over our heads. It was a powerful sight. That evening, Nathalie drew her first picture using colored pencils, and it portrayed birds in different colors covering the whole sheet of paper. Needless to say, I still have this picture, nicely framed and prominently displayed. Both girls liked drawing and painting. Lydia was more into color, and Nathalie concentrated on movement. They made illustrations based on books they read, painted country landscapes, countless fruit bowls, and vases with flowers. Sometimes, I would join them.

During the summer months, before their camp program started, I would often take the girls to Central Park to Rollerblade, play badminton or bocci. After having circled the neighboring streets for a few minutes, we would usually find a parking spot within a reasonable distance and would happily trot to the park. Very often, we would stop at the Metropolitan Museum of Art to check some of the works we especially liked and to sketch some painting or other. To this day I regret having lost Nathalie's pencil sketch of Archangel Gabriel, which I particularly liked. She made it casually on a reverse side of some notebook, and I must have inadvertently thrown it out.

I often brought the girls to numerous art exhibitions and encouraged them to copy the paintings they saw. Once I took them, preschoolers at the time, to an exhibition of a well-known contemporary artist. When we were already in the hallway and about to leave the premises of the museum, a commotion began. It turned out that the artist himself had shown up briefly to sign the exhibition catalogs. The room filled quickly with people. We were relegated to the farthest corner of the room, and I was standing there, clutching my catalog, unwilling to leave, yet realizing there was no way I could reach the artist across this human sea with my two little ones in their bulky winter coats. All of a sudden, without saying a word, a man grabbed my catalog. The next thing I knew my booklet was moving along to the front of the crowd, undulating gently as it changed hands. The artist was smiling while he signed it. In under a minute, I had it back. How I regretted that the girls were too young to put this moment into the jewel box of their most precious memories.

Both our daughters are quite musically gifted. Lydia has perfect pitch, and Nathalie's pitch is almost as good. On top of that, Lydia's hand was considered to be very well shaped for a piano player from the very beginning. As is often the case, since I am not very gifted myself, it made me especially proud, in my vain parental moments, when I took our six-year-old Lydia to piano recitals. I would ask her carelessly what was the tonality of the work being performed and she would reply very matter-of-factly, without pausing for more than a few seconds. Of course, I was probably the only one impressed, because people who attend classical music concerts usually take such prowess for granted. There is a limit to everything, so I did not dare drag the then three-year-old Nathalie to concert halls with us.

Despite their natural talent, they did not practice enough to pursue professional musical careers from the very beginning. They did enjoy their classes, but I did not see any special interest on their part, that telling spark in their eyes that would signify outstanding talent which would push its way through to the fore and guarantee that was the right path for them. So I decided on one hour a day, which seemed enough to introduce the girls to the world of music and instill good technique, yet not interfere with the rest of the educational process. Our first teacher was actually quite shocked when I told her that they were only practicing for one hour a day; she thought the girls practiced much more.

I was aware from the very beginning that professional musical training required a totally different approach. One story was discussed especially vividly among parents during the acceptance exams to the music school. It made waves because it addressed the key concern of most parents. One boy did very well and was praised profusely by his teachers. When, upon his graduation, his parents mentioned an interest in a musical career for him, the teachers couldn't hide their surprise. They did not realize professional interest was present. The parents were told that their boy should have had a stricter regimen and a more difficult repertoire if he was considering choosing music as his career. As it was, he was judged and praised based on criteria for amateurs.

The piano lessons were something Alex disapproved of. He saw no practical need for them and thought it was a waste of time and money, as we were not considering musical careers for our girls. Alex's distaste for music education makes his eventual support that much more precious. When the time came to decide whether to buy or rent a piano, I suggested buying a baby grand, to make the lessons more special. We certainly could not afford it at that time. We did not even have a car yet. Alex agreed nonetheless to buy it, further putting off purchasing a car. Even if this was the only thing he ever did for me and our daughters, it would have been enough for me.

At first, our music teacher looked at us with suspicion and even with a touch of outright unfriendliness. She did not expect anything good, at least not anytime soon, from a pupil who came to her lessons with a small bench to put under her feet so that her feet didn't dangle while she played. In a year, Lydia became her best student and was eventually joined by Nathalie, who, as a result, had a much easier time being acknowledged. This was very fortunate, considering that Nathalie, who was four, one year younger than Lydia was when she began her musical studies, not only needed the bench, but her hand was so small she could barely make a five-note chord. Very soon they were playing four-hand duets and we all had a great time attending these classes and school concerts

Once, when we arrived to the lesson, we heard beautiful music coming from our classroom. We carefully opened the door just a little and took a peek. Our teacher was playing. Her eyes shining and her cheeks pink with excitement, she was very different from the composed strict lady I had come to know. She later told me that our ardor and the energy that emanated from our small bunch inspired her to go back and play piano for fun again.

The girls took piano lessons until they left for college. Once, Nathalie's friends came over after school. Many of them played, others were just interested in the grand piano. They crowded around the instrument and took turns playing. I left them alone and went into my room. Suddenly, I heard the sonatina Nathalie was working on at the time. The piece was being played with no feeling, no nuances. It was just senseless tapping on the keys. Immediately, I felt devastated. Maybe their lessons were a waste of time after all. I peeked out of my room. It was not Nathalie. I felt so ashamed for even thinking it could have been her, for jumping to conclusions so fast without even giving her the benefit of a doubt. I should have known better. I felt like I betrayed her. But I felt relieved, too. When in a few minutes it was Nathalie's turn, I heard what I was hoping to hear. She felt and understood the piece. It was not a waste of time.

***

I did not forget about sports. I was never much into competitive sports myself. Only when my body started to age and it became more and more difficult to make it bend a little further or walk an extra mile did I start to find not only pure fun but challenge, and as a result, a special interest in sporting activities. According to my plan, sports were assigned the task of stimulating the development of the girls' bodies, of making them healthy, strong, and beautiful. I also had been hearing the dictum, *In corpus sano spiritus sanum*—a healthy mind in a healthy body—since I was a child.

My lax attitude toward competitive sports was once the cause of a huge parental mistake on my part. Nathalie, already a volleyball varsity team member, came home very excited one day and announced that she received the Most Valuable Player award. Not to justify myself, but to use as an extenuating circumstance, Lydia, like a typical teenager, did not insist on my presence at her sporting events, and even though she was very good and had already received a few awards, kept a low profile. So, after praising Nathalie very briefly, I told her that I was busy helping Lydia get ready for a math test. Lydia had an international baccalaureate course in math, and it was not easy. Besides, I always liked math myself and thought it to be one of the most important school subjects. I have always felt it was a sort of shorthand for all of life's experiences, the most succinct and precise language of all. I must have sounded very dismissive. Nathalie still remembers my gaffe. I did correct my ways almost immediately, however.

From that time on, I attended the girls' games, mostly Nathalie's, and even cheered for them. My rooting technique was another story altogether. It exasperated and made the girls laugh at the same time. In their eyes, it was tepid, to say the least. I did not shout, stomp on the floor, or God forbid, whistle. I knew they were right, but it was not because I did not want them to win. It was just that my upbringing mandated not showing my emotions and it proved quite difficult to disregard. At least I was there for them. And I still keep all of their individual and team trophies.

Both Lydia and Nathalie learned to swim very early. They skied, ran, Rollerbladed, bicycled, bowled, played badminton, tennis, table tennis, bocci, mini-golf, and billiards. They were both on junior varsity and varsity teams when they grew up. Lydia played volleyball and basketball, and Nathalie played volleyball and was on a track and field team. In college, Lydia was on the sailing team. Nathalie joined a club rugby team her freshman year, against her better judgment and my advice. They also took ice-skating lessons as preschoolers.

I put the girls on skates almost as soon as they could walk. Actually, maybe slightly before, in Nathalie's case, since I took her to her first lessons in a stroller. At first, I took the girls to a group that was certainly not geared toward professional ice-skating. A nice, slightly overweight woman ran the class. Everything went fine in the beginning, while the kids were working on the basics, the forward and the backward steps and some other key elements. Very soon it became apparent that it was a waste of time and not going anywhere. It felt like a cozy tea party one lazy summer afternoon. The lady, though very good with the children, was lifeless. She had no stamina, no focus, no real interest in what she was doing. Most importantly, she was not particularly invested in getting the kids interested in what *they* were doing. Actually, I was afraid that it was not only useless but pernicious. There was a big chance the girls would get bored and lose any desire to continue with their lessons. We managed to escape that time, but we still did have one similar experience down the road.

Since Nathalie was three years old, she wanted to be a ballerina. I do not remember how it all started. All I know is that she is the only person, let alone child, that I have ever met, who could endure watching ballet on television and actually enjoy it. For almost three years, she never wore regular slippers at home, only real pointe shoes. She went through dozens of them. When she was five, a new pair of said pointe shoes and a brand new pink tutu stuffed in her special pink bag, she departed for her first ballet class. She was expecting a miracle. It ended in disaster. She got so bored lifting and lowering her leg for practically the entire length of the lesson, she never even spoke about ballet again. She discarded her pointe shoes the same day, and did not want to discuss any more classes. She never became a ballerina, but she is a great dancer, tirelessly keeping the center stage spot at every party from beginning to end. I do believe that true talent finds its way, no matter what, as water seeps through the soil, so probably it was just as well, but I am sad nonetheless for things that could have been, of experiences that could have been acquired, of memories that could have been shared.

Back to the ice-skating, however. Almost two months went by, Lydia turned six. I was lamenting the state of affairs in the group and was looking for an alternative. That was when a friend of mine recommended a pilot project for a group of preschoolers taught by a former ballet-on-ice professional. The lessons took place five days a week and lasted four hours. Once the children started school, they were supposed to take the same classes after regular school hours. Lydia was accepted into the group and Nathalie was allowed to attend as long as she stayed in the corner of the rink out of everybody's way and just tried to emulate the older kids.

Nowhere was my approach more at odds with the predominant attitude than in this ice-skating group. As a child, I never engaged in any serious sporting activity, so the tyranny of professional training was a novel concept for me.

After a few weeks' worth of lessons, I was approached by the coach. The group was divided into two subgroups, according to ability. Lydia, who started in the lower subgroup, was showing promise, and the coach transferred her into the higher one. This fact was lost on Lydia, who did not show any excitement and continued working in the same regime, and I did not pressure her to work harder. Very nicely and diplomatically, the coach told me that I was too soft on the girls, and that they would never achieve great results if I did not change my attitude. I could barely hide my astonishment. The idea of conscientious, continuous bossing of children as a means of promoting excellence was absolutely unacceptable to me. I was very careful to avoid a lengthy philosophical discussion on this subject, however, and got off the hook by some hypocritical promises.

Strictly speaking, the group was not professional, but the seriousness of the lessons implied it. Indeed, most parents around me saw ice-skating as a ticket to a successful life for their children. Parents were always hovering on the edge of the rink, monitoring their child's every movement. They were practically drilling the ice under their children's feet with their eyes, commenting and correcting their technique along with the coach. Not all of them were entertaining ideas of a professional skating future for their kids, but even those who did not felt that they should push with all their might to get the best possible results, or not do it at all. The atmosphere was pretty heated. Actually, many parents of the kids in our painting and music classes felt the same way.

Shortly after my talk with the coach, my unorthodox ways in the world of serious sports became the cause of a standoff during one of these ice-skating classes. Usually I would stand with everybody else. Speeds were high, blades were sharp. I became convinced that it was my being there with my eyes glued to Lydia's feet that kept her safe. When a few weeks had passed without any trouble, I decided to make another attempt to go back to my studies and try to write my thesis paper, after all. I lugged a bag full of books to the class with me (notebooks were not yet available), and while everybody was at the rink, sneaked out and spread my papers on the floor in the empty gym. I did not work for long. One of the fathers, who happened to pass by the gym, accosted me right then and there and accused me of being too soft on the girls and too meek, depriving my children of a bright future and of being a callous, selfish nitwit, to add insult to injury. He also pointed out that I was not instilling the right attitude toward work in my girls. He was not diplomatic at all. I did not say much after he was through with his unwarranted contumely. I did not feel like explaining myself to him. In any event, he was obviously very set in his own beliefs, and I doubted he would see my point and understand that it was not oblivious aloofness on my part.

I had a very different outlook on this matter of cultural and sportive euthanasia. Go all the way or not at all. Why? Why this need for a practical outcome, why such a pragmatic approach to the sources of great spiritual and physical pleasure?

The fine line here is showing respect toward what you are doing and the desire to do it right, but also respect for the child. How far you go along the right track depends upon your ability and the amount of time you want to dedicate to it, and ultimately, what role this activity is supposed to play in your life.

I had a tuner over to our house once, a very old man. After he had finished tuning the instrument, I offered him some tea. We were chatting, and he told me a story. He was asked once to come tune a piano by the parents of a little boy. They were very perplexed as to why the keys of their brand new instrument got stuck so often. As the tuner soon learned, there was nothing wrong with the instrument. The keys were glued together by jam. It turned out the boy was eating sandwiches while practicing.

Besides talent, success in arts, music, or sports requires a huge time commitment and necessarily must happen at the expense of something else. From very early on, children grow up oriented predominantly in one direction. If parents push their children too hard, often compensating for talent by time invested in the activity, such individuals may become less harmonious beings, like growths with just one stick of what you perceived to be of the paramount importance instead of a beautiful tree, with many branches and a full crown. Such children may also have forever missed other opportunities, which could have been a better fit for them.

In addition, only very few succeed. Actually, nowhere is the outcome as iffy as in sports. Sports, being the epitome of competition—competition at its purest—requires much more than just talent and hard work. They require an even higher level of drive, ambition, physical strength and endurance, stress management skills, and just pure luck, compared with other endeavors.

Was this father sure that his daughter's talent was as outstanding as he imagined and hoped it to be, or was it just his wishful thinking? Was he so sure her ambitions would equal his, that his daughter would pick up where he left off? And that even if she were successful, it was really her true calling, and not his dream, and that it would make her happy?

I went back to the rink, however, and never tried to work on my thesis during the classes again. But this was not because of that father's intervention. While I was away, Lydia fell pretty badly, which reinforced my original belief that my presence made a difference.

For the final celebratory event before summer vacation, I knitted Lydia a snowflake costume. I took to knitting a few years prior, when the girls were still very young. Every day was so much like the previous one. Life seemed to go in circles, and I needed some tangible proof of its progress.

I had no pattern to work from, but it was one of my best creations. Half blue and half white, with a little skirt, it fitted Lydia like a glove. It took me longer to knit it than I anticipated, and I did not sleep the night before the event. I finished a few minutes before it was time to wake the girls, but a sleepless night was no longer an issue by that time. Lydia was happy. After the festivities, I told the coach and the parents that I was pulling Lydia out of the group when she started regular school.

If Lydia were to remain in the group, it would have to become her only extracurricular activity. She would have to give up her art and music lessons. I could not make such an important decision for my child in an arbitrary fashion, when she was just six years old. I was not afraid to make a decision, but realizing the huge power parents can wield over their young child's destiny made me especially cautious in using it.

To me, it held enormous risk. The probability that the girls had enough talent and other qualities required to succeed in a sport, or music or arts, for that matter, seemed small to me, regardless of the fact that I was pushed by many teachers (except our first art teacher, who did not push anyone) to consider such careers for the girls. I did not want to risk it. The girls enjoyed all their classes, but they were not particularly thrilled by them. The required dedication would be justified only if it had an interest to match. Pure mathematics, as always.

But this was only partially the reason. I can see that it could be argued that such a coercive approach is a good way to teach children to live in our competitive world, and that even if the child does not achieve any substantial success, at least she or he would have acquired the skills useful to succeed in any other field. The veracity of this contention notwithstanding, I just did not have what it took to force our children to such an extent.

I considered myself a strict mother. I had never encouraged a laissez-faire attitude. I would have fainted if the girls did not put their hands on the piano the correct way or did not stand on the ice in their pretty white skates as if they were glued to it at the right angle, without wobbling, but I did not expect them to play Rachmaninov's Piano Concerto No. 3 or do a triple axel, unless this was what they wanted. I have to admit, however, that

I would have never risked killing enthusiasm when I saw it in the girls' eyes by enforcing the right way of doing things from the very beginning. I have always preferred to first secure and reinforce genuine interest over proper skills. When you start to insist on all or nothing right away, you wind up with nothing more often than not, and such an outcome was precisely what I was trying to avoid.

All of our involvement with the arts, music, and sports felt more like coming to a theater late at night, after the performance was already over and the next one was a whole day away. You go backstage, try on professional makeup, and maybe even get a nod of approval from a great master, exigent but benevolent, after reading him your favorite monologue. I did not want our girls to be in the limelight during the next performance, not just yet, but to know the inner workings of the craft to allow them to enjoy and understand it better.

This father's approach reminded me very much of an arranged marriage. In my opinion, there is no difference between marrying a person or a profession without love. By doing so, we snuff out the most precious internal source of our own energy and happiness.

I can do something I do not like to appease a tyrant, support an insecure person, or just because I like somebody, but in matters affecting our deep inner structure I value personal freedom above all else. To be truly happy, every human being must have a song. But as with the famous nightingale, the soul does not sing in captivity. I, for my part, could not even train a bonsai tree.

I became fascinated at some point by the beauty of bonsai trees after attending an exhibition. I purchased one. I also purchased a how-to book. I realized I would have to wire branches and slowly bend and twist them into the desired shape and cut the superfluous ones out altogether. I just could not make myself do it. Is it at all surprising that I rebelled against doing it to our children?

The funny thing is, internal freedom requires a lot of hard work, a very strict regimen, and numerous restrictions. Freedom is not doing whatever you may fancy at any given moment. Internal freedom is having a sufficient command of your environment to lessen its pressure on you. Freedom means knowing how to achieve what you want, without infringing on other people's rights, of course. Freedom is to know how to survive and to succeed in this world. A great athlete is free in terms of being able to sustain a lot of physical pressure and hard work for a long time, but it comes at a price. He has to train himself religiously, and is bound by a rigorous exercise routine and diet. A healthy diet and exercise make us strong and free of many ailments, these being the laws of dialectics. It is only natural that Hegel's definition of freedom became my motto, that is, "Freedom is the recognition of necessity."

I was aware that "Success," to quote the famous formula by Thomas Edison, "is ten percent inspiration and ninety percent perspiration." I was never deterred by hard work. I knew that one had to work hard even if they had talent, actually, *especially* if they had talent, because working in a field you have no propensity for is ultimately useless. It was the principle of breaking children into submission, the infinite power of parents over their children I rebelled against. The principle that parents always know best. To raise a human being one has to start with respect for that human being— respect for the child—his or her inner world, his or her personal inclinations and proclivities.

This sounds like a sacrilegious thought, but in the world of fast change parents can no longer know best. Not that long ago, historically speaking, a diligent parent would give his son into apprenticeship and feel secure that although his child's life would probably be extremely hard during those years, he would have mastered a skill, as a result, that would allow him to survive. His father did it, and so did the father of his father. Things have changed dramatically since then. Thanks to the galloping development of new technologies, there is no way of knowing what new occupations the marketplace will require five years from now, let alone by the time our preschoolers graduate. Occupations like android and iOS developer, social media scientist, market research data miner, or chief listening officer did not even exist ten years ago. On the other hand, many careers like telephone operators or film processors have disappeared.

Figure-skating will probably be with us for some time, but Zumba instructors did not exist ten years ago.

Chapter Fourteen

When Nathalie was three years old, she loved cats. Once, quite by accident, we saw a lady who was selling very small kittens, probably two or three days old. Nathalie got excited and wanted one so badly, I bought her one. Her joy was enormous. All the way home she held him tight against her chest. When at home, she made him a bed and tried to put him to sleep. Not surprisingly, the kitten had no desire to sleep in the middle of the day and no desire to comply with the whims of a baby human either. Disappointed but not deterred, Nathalie tried to feed him. He was not very receptive to that either. My attempts to convince Nathalie to let the poor soul be were ignored. Instead, Nathalie started to get a little annoyed at the lack of cooperation and resumed her attempts to put the kitten to bed. At this point, the little creature lost his patience. I saw the paws stiffen and slowly release tiny claws. I grabbed the girls and rushed back to the market to return the kitten to his owner. Luckily, the lady was still around.

Nathalie was inconsolable for a few days after this incident, but then she diverted her attention to our neighbor's cat. She would pick him up and go sit with him for a very long time, petting him while holding him on her knees. The moment the cat tried to escape, however, the caressing hand would firmly bring him back. The cat was patient and understanding for many days. But finally he lost it. One fine morning I saw Nathalie running straight through the bushes, the cat chasing her, this picturesque sight accompanied by an awful hubbub of branches being broken, the cat's meowing, and Nathalie screaming. Maybe these unsuccessful attempts at securing feline friendship had something to do with the fact that Nathalie loves dogs now.

Even from a practical point of view, I think that the method of forcing children to work in a particular field is flawed. I knew from my own experience that no one could make me work harder than myself, no one knew better than me how to trick myself into high gear. No one can push you further than you will push yourself if you move on your own desire and ability. To wake up a genuine interest in the girls seemed like a much more reasonable way to produce results. I do not particularly like the surrealist painter, Rene Magritte, but I think nothing sums up the child-rearing process better than his painting, *Clairvoyance*. I figured that my goal as a parent was to find, nurture, and unleash our children's potential.

My premise was that the child has to love what he or she does, and we all usually love what we are good at. So, first, parents should help their children find what they love, find their strengths, inclinations, and talents. Parents should help light a fire from the internal pilot flame, being very careful not to extinguish it, to start the engine. But the drive has to come from within.

My method was still to expose them to as many different activities and stimuli as possible and to see what excited them. This way, I was not arbitrarily narrowing the array of their potential choices, I was widening it so they could choose their true calling when the time came. All the while, I tried to proceed with care, mindful first and foremost not to break them. Broken souls are like broken instruments. They are incapable of producing a beautiful melody.

It seems to me that life is a journey on a river as you swim against the current, from the estuary to the source. In the beginning, you have a tremendous amount of energy and a lot of opportunities. As your life goes on, you swim upstream, following one tributary or another, to continue with the analogy, as you make your life choices. Your energy level declines, your river becomes narrower, as your choices narrow down your opportunities. If you choose wisely, you come to your own source. If not, you begin to knock along banks and feel constrained. It is very important to find your own beginnings, your own true self. Only then can one feel comfortable and satisfied, and happy.

I wanted to prepare our children to make the right choices, not to make choices for them. Children are like safe-boxes to me. You have to find an individual key to every human being. You have to try and try again until you hear that clicking sound and the door to the child's soul opens. What a huge moral responsibility to be entrusted with a human life, however. Our children love and trust us. More than anything else, I was afraid of not being worthy of our daughters' trust. There is such a fine line between help and manipulation. I always had to remember to promote their interests, their goals, not my own. Parents are guardians, not guards.

Every child is terra incognita, just like a new country. It is so exciting to explore them, to find out all the obvious and out-of-the-beaten-path treasures. I was trying to look at our children with an open mind, with no preconceptions. Just as when I was traveling in some faraway exotic land, I did not start looking for a McDonalds or Starbucks right away, or failing to find one, be compelled to build one. One of the most important questions is, precisely, how much is innate and to what extent can we alter nature? Can nurture override nature in the nature versus nurture debate, or is the environment bound to only reinforce or weaken what is already there? Is a child like a grain and parents like the farmers who can raise an abundant crop, with a little luck if they work diligently, prepare the soil well, plant at the right time, and water and fertilize properly? Or are we more like artists? Is our new baby more like an amorphous piece of clay, with certain innate qualities, granted, but still offering us substantial creative possibilities?

Can we change the matrix, in other words, or can our efforts only produce quantitative changes? It looked like we would not be able to change lead into gold anytime soon, at any event, but that there might be ranges of possibilities to find out and explore. Clearer understanding still eluded me, but I had a tantalizing feeling that the answer was already in the offing.

Despite my brush-off of the righteous father, I was more shaken than I wanted to admit. At night, I would lie in my bed, unable to sleep, feeling small and lonely, looking at the dark sky through the open window. I needed some reassurance, and I was hoping for some validation of my methods. Truly, those who seek shall find. It came from unexpected yet very logical quarters, come to think of it.

When I was in my teens, my mother gave me a book, *Stone and Pain*, about Michelangelo. I got interested in him and other artists of the Renaissance era after having seen so much of their work. I have always liked to read about artists since that first unforgettable book.

I came across an article about Michelangelo in one of the old magazines I was flipping through one last time before throwing it out. The article quoted Michelangelo's definition of sculpture as the art of "taking away," not that of "adding on." He believed that the form was already imprisoned in the stone and only needed to be discovered by the artist by taking away the superfluous and unnecessary in order to free this form. My hands started to tremble. How could I forget? That was it. That was the magic formula. So I found myself a powerful paladin. No wonder Michelangelo was obsessed with finding the right marble block. Not every block could hide a *David* or a *Pieta,* and parents, of course, do not have Carrara quarries at their disposal. We have to work with what we've got.

In a way, this concept is also in keeping with the most important rule of medicine—*Do no harm.* Better to shave off less than to cut into living flesh. This is a human being, a living organism, and also a system, meaning everything is interconnected, one trait is supported by others, and on the other hand, feeds and supports many other traits. One can't just yank something from a human personality. The person may crumble like a cardhouse.

***

All of my vague thoughts and ideas fell into one congruous conception. Raising children is a creative process. The child is not a clean slate, however. For a human being to create, he or she must reveal what is already there, to uncover nature's design, and to resist our vain human urges to clone ourselves or to follow our whims. We should not destroy and then mold something totally foreign and unnatural, but eliminate the superfluous, carefully take off the excess, not twist and bend our children into the wrong shape and form. We have to set free the true nature, while at the same time carefully and gently suppressing the undesirable and nurturing the desirable. Not every child has the potential to become Einstein or Michelangelo, but if we release the hidden idea, if we are talented artists, that is, our child has a good chance to be as beautiful a creation as she or he can be.

It is said, "like father, like son," that "the apple does not fall far from the tree." This approach, however, may theoretically provide a great opportunity to make your apple tree bear oranges by not preventing the growth of something that can not only be bigger and better than you, but also different from you.

To achieve this goal is our challenge as parents.

One cannot but realize, pondering these questions, that special knowledge would be extremely helpful for being a good parent. Which, of course, only a few parents have. Then again, nature could not have anticipated parents having degrees in pedagogy to have healthy, happy, and successful progeny. Or enjoying equal financial opportunities, for that matter. There must be an instrument within everyone's reach, be it a financial magnate or a poor farmer, a university professor or a high-school dropout.

I have wondered for a long time whether nature can offset the tremendous differences in children's initial social and financial opportunities. I think that giving us the gift of parental love is as close as nature gets to fairness. We are all equal in that we possess this tool, the ability to love. No rich or poor here. Theoretically, parental love should be then the most important survival tool. It may probably never fully bridge the gap between those who have lucked out and those who have not, but it can probably narrow the playing field by making perception more acute, and by thus allowing us to fish out and nurture every bit of talent. It gives us the required insight, wisdom, patience, and kindness. A child is a custom-made product, fine-tuned all the time. Different children, different parents, and different environment require different demands and different methods. Love is a chisel or a magic wand, if you prefer to think of it that way. I prefer the chisel. And, while making sure every child becomes the best he or she can be, in the meantime, parental love should also make sure that every child is growing up happy.

For the thousands of years that men have existed, nature, it seems, has created a mechanism to be sure the helpless human babies are taken care of. I also think that children have a built-in resilience and wisdom to withstand a lot of parental mistakes, provided they are done by a loving mother or father. We are all bound to be parents for the first time, there is no realistic way of mastering the subject beforehand. Children certainly do suffer from parental mistakes, but not nearly as badly as from parental neglect or parental betrayal.

Nature may have devised a brilliant master plan, but it is so easy to mess things up. We are, alas, only human. The world around us is not cruel. It is unbiased and objective to the point of cruelty. So, the only way to win the battle of life would require observing our children with equally objective eyes. Love then should not be the Stendhal's blinding crystallization. Love should help us to see the true nature of our child, not a sugar-coated image. Only an objective, true assessment of the child's capabilities can help us come up with a perfect fit between our expectations and the child's abilities. This is no small feat.

One of the biggest challenges in life is probably to see and accept ourselves and our children for what they really are. The pressure from the outside is tremendous. We are supposed to be smart, beautiful, thin, well-read, well-mannered, charming, and sexy. The list goes on and on. G.B. Shaw once said, "You don't find yourself, you create yourself." I am not sure I fully agree. Instead, you must painstakingly grow yourself, like all things in nature. You have to find your grain and grow the appropriate plant. We may partly implant some more or less exotic trait into our core, like some good geneticists do, but there are surely limitations to what our body and soul would accept and what they would reject as absolutely foreign, the same way it is not possible to cross cows with horses for a viable species.

I do believe it is possible to rise above our limitations by a huge willpower tour de force, but could such imposition of artificial growth bring happiness? Wouldn't all such connections be forced, unnatural, painful? A much more rewarding way would be to try not to overlook and to nurture existing abilities. The gauge of my success as a parent should not then be our children's high achievements, per se, but the full realization of their initial potential. I tried not to impose arbitrarily high expectations, but to have esteem for our girls' inclinations and capabilities, providing a loving and nurturing family atmosphere all the while. And then, I believed, a miracle could happen, for every child is unique and priceless, like a work of art. I just had to follow Michelangelo's advice.

Still, I was worried that my nebulous, highfalutin constructions based on the ideas of Renaissance artists and the Enlightenment philosophers may not be very well suited for life in the twenty-first century. Were my emerging theories like castles on the sand, like beautiful mirages in the desert?

One Saturday evening, as was our custom at the time, we went to a Chinese restaurant, which were so ubiquitous in New York in the late eighties. After the meal, I cracked open my fortune cookie and read my fortune, as usual. It said, "Doing what you love is freedom. Loving what you do is happiness." I took this as a final stamp of approval of my methods. At that point, I considered my research complete. For some time, at least. At last, I had a tuning device, a valid strategy, and a cynosure. As for the tuning...as with any musical instrument, tuning is not a once-in-a-lifetime occurrence. We have to stay on our toes.

Chapter Fifteen

One of the most important decisions parents have to face is the school we choose for our children. This decision was made by us practically overnight. We went with UNIS, the United Nations International School. It happened quite naturally, and in hindsight, proved to be a truly serendipitous choice. The children of most of our friends and acquaintances went there and they had nothing but positive feedback. The school offered the International Baccalaureate program, the IB. That fact made it very appealing to the international community of the UN employees, whose kids often went on to get their higher degrees in their respective countries, and the IB smoothed the transition. French was offered in elementary school as a second language, which was a big draw for me. And last but not least, the school practically sat in our backyard. This proximity allowed our girls to have more time after classes to get things gone, to get more sleep, and to have a good breakfast.

Another saying I heard very often from my father was, "Eat the breakfast yourself, share lunch with your friend, give your dinner to your enemy." Funnily, to look at the New York dining scene, one could assume that either its dwellers are a bunch of perfidious, conniving people set to feed each other to death, or that they are happily oblivious of this school of thought. Twenty years ago our friend, a cafe owner, used to lament the decreasing interest in eating out during the times of economic recessions. Apparently, things have changed dramatically nowadays, judging by the fact that even during the toughest months of the latest crash, Alex and I once had to try five or six local cafes on a weekday, before finding a free spot.

***

A good breakfast was one of my small obsessions. My little babies, still very warm after a good night's sleep, had to have a hot meal, be it oatmeal, Cream of Wheat, or the girls' absolute favorite, pancakes. I was not looking for shortcuts and would not allow myself to cut any corners. There was no Aunt Jemima for me. I made the pancake batter from scratch, which was very easy to do anyway, truth be told.

History seemed to be repeating itself. I did not want to let go of the Russian school curriculum. The scheme of weekend and evening studies was quickly put into place. The Russian curriculum was different from its American counterpart and more demanding. It obviously also included the Russian language and Russian literature, so I had to make sure that our girls did not fall behind and would be able to smoothly integrate into the Russian system when the time came to return to Moscow.

I incorporated the Russian literature curriculum into our evening readings. I must admit, however, that I had much more fun reading these books than my girls did listening because most of them were intended for a much more mature audience. Well, I certainly took advantage of that unexpected second chance at a trove of wonderful treasures, and made a mental note to reread many other books I thought I remembered.

I did not want our children to go to school just to learn to speak English and breeze through all the other subjects, just as I did not want to just learn to speak decent French when I was studying in Geneva. So I came to the school introductory meeting with a notepad and a pen, ready to jot down the precious nuggets of wisdom that would allow me to fully benefit from the American educational system. Two things shocked me right away at that very first school gathering—food and jokes.

One of the ways the school took advantage of the diversity of its student body was through food. No gathering, big or small, was held without a buffet of international dishes whisked up by the industrious students' mothers. To nibble on a piece of home-baked bread smothered with some delicious spread while listening to the school policy on dress code or any such topic was unusual, to say the least.

There was another matter that was equally disturbing—jokes. I was not prepared for the ubiquitous and constant use of this piece of rhetoric weaponry in school surroundings. I was shocked and alarmed. It was a totally different and unknown culture.

Years later, I started driving regularly to Washington, DC to visit our daughters. I usually took the George Washington Memorial Parkway, and after crossing the Key Bridge, was entering the orderly and unhurriedly polite streets of the capital. After New York City, where taxi drivers would honk at you one split second before the light turned green, and where it was a matter of principle not to let anybody cut in front of you, practically a standard procedure adopted by pedestrians nowadays as well, I needed some time to readjust. I used to laugh at myself, mentally comparing my attitude to that of a street cat ready for a fight, hair on end, back arched, transported all of a sudden into a nice elegant house. Looking back now, I perceive myself the same way at the time of my first class meetings. The analogy did not come to my mind then, however. I was too tense in the unfamiliar environment, not knowing what to expect, too concentrated on not missing anything important in my determination to help our children succeed.

I came home with a clean notepad, not counting a small piece of a scone that got pressed between its pages. It must have fallen when I was laughing at one of the jokes. I did not want to jump to any conclusions, but one thing was obvious: I had a lot of hard work ahead.

Practically the next day after our girls started school and I got to meet my friends' children on the school premises, and not on the playground with their mothers present, I was shocked at how impolite they all were. I grew up knowing that whatever I could forget to do, I should never forget to greet my elders. None said hello to me, and would just zip by hurriedly. This bothered me quite a lot. I sensed that something was not right, that I was missing something. Then, I remembered. Of course! Speak when spoken to. Perfectly brought up, these kids were waiting for me to address them.

All my love for strategies and grand schemes of life notwithstanding, many of my decisions, especially when the girls were very young, were done if not for the explicitly wrong reasons, but definitely for rather peculiar ones. They usually worked out quite fine in the end, but the fact remains.

When Nathalie was about to start school, we had a choice. She was born in December, so she could, theoretically, go straight into the first grade and skip kindergarten. When I brought her in for an interview, the school representative voiced some doubts as to whether it was reasonable to have her skip a year. I was leaning toward first grade—why waste one year?—but my mind was not definitely made up yet.

I did not prepare the girls for school purposefully, but by age five and a half, Nathalie was already what would later be referred to on report cards and resumes as an avid reader. After her interview, the school representatives had no more doubts, and did not object to enrolling her in the first grade. During her interview, one of the other schoolteachers showed me around. At some point, we peeked into a big room with closed blinds where twenty or so children were lying on the floor wrapped up in their blankets. The lady proudly explained that this was where kindergarten children took their nap time, a practice that was abandoned in the first grade. Dear UNIS, please forgive me, but this sight horrified me. For my child to sleep on the hard, cold floor, and not in her cozy bed, on her favorite Ninja Turtles sheets? And during school hours? No way. My mind was made up then and there.

The advantages of starting school early are open to debate. In fact, nowadays, red-shirting is more common, at least amongst the Upper East Side elite who seek to give their children a competitive edge. It certainly depends on many factors, and since there are no ifs in history, they are hard to assess. The decision that I consider unequivocally beneficial, however, was my becoming a class mother. It helped me a lot in catching quite a few of those nuggets of wisdom I was so desperately searching for. Indeed, God works in mysterious ways.

***

School trips scared me to death. I dreaded the very thought of them from the minute I learned one was scheduled. I had trouble falling asleep the night before, thinking of everything that might go wrong. The only solution I could think of to ease my stress was to be with my kids. I became a class mother. This decision did not come naturally. I grew up harboring a slight mistrust and a great dislike of active parents. My mother, being quite shy by nature, did not go to school unless she absolutely had to, and I had heard many times that my grandmother Olga, not shy at all, considered it futile in general and rarely attended school gatherings either.

I still can't think about my first class trip without a shudder. I don't think I ever had a worst headache than after I crawled out of the school bus that day. The yelling and shouting were atrocious. The decibel level certainly surpassed by a wide margin the one that the health gurus deemed acceptable. What amazed me the most was that the teacher did not seem disconcerted in the least, and was just merrily walking up and down the aisle, making sure the kids remained seated.

I did not want to fall into what I saw as one of the major pitfalls as far as the children's upbringing was concerned, that is, to suffocate children with love, to be too overbearing and overprotective, a helicopter mom. I came to think that not to allow the child to do reasonable things out of fear was a form of selfishness, not love, that shutting the child away from the world for whatever reason, be it out of fear or out of a more reasonable desire to protect taken to unreasonable levels is as detrimental as being overly permissive.

As scary as it was for me to let the girls go, I felt I had to start the process. From playdates to sleepovers, to trips with friends around the country, and ultimately around the world. I remember one year our daughters were ringing in the New Year, one in Vienna, and the other in Melbourne, and I don't mean Vienna, Virginia or Melbourne, Florida. They were already college students by then, however.

School ushered in a whole plethora of new issues to deal with. When our children were young, they did not interact very much with the environment. Alex and I were their entire universe. Now the environment was pushing through and entering into the limelight. Should I control this process, and if so, to what extent? How much should I allow, and what parts should I allow? What would be the right balance?

I was still debating these issues when the Soviet Union collapsed in December 1991. Lydia was in the fourth grade and Nathalie in second.

***

The unsurmountable ideological divide between Russia and the West ceased to exist. The Iron Curtain crumbled. It meant different things to different people. My personal wall started to disintegrate much earlier, and was not at all a solid monolith by that time.

The Cold War was going into the detente phase when I was old enough to register the ideological differences between the Soviet Union and the West, but it was certainly very early in the spring yet. As a Soviet child, and later, as a Soviet woman abroad, I have witnessed some downright hostile attitudes, but also a lot of friendliness and help. As a means of making sense of this duality, I began, involuntarily and almost subconsciously, to search for a unifying element that would make constructive interaction possible, or more precisely, to explain to myself why the ideological friend-or-foe system so often malfunctioned on a personal level and why such interaction was at all possible. Instinctively, I started to delve into deeper layers of the human personality, and as a result, over time, to perceive the main gauge for such interactions not as an ideological but as an ethical one. Having traveled this road myself, I once recognized the signs of the onset of the longing for common ground and continuity in my five-year-old daughter's deliberations.

We used to go to Russia on vacation about once a year, but there was a longer break when I was pregnant with Nathalie and when Nathalie was a baby. So Lydia came to Moscow when she had just turned five after a break of more than two years. The security guards in our apartment complex in New York, who were usually present near the playground, wore navy uniforms not unlike the uniforms of the Russian militiamen. Once, when we went into an underpass to cross a wide avenue, Lydia noticed one such militiaman, and, happy to spot at least one remotely familiar figure, shouted gleefully, "Mom, a guard!" By unfortunate coincidence, the word guard sounds very much like the Russian word for *scumbag*. "Mom" being an international word, the phrase sounded in Russian roughly like, "Mom, a scumbag!" The sound carried particularly well in the long underpass.

I froze in fear, thinking feverishly how I would explain why my kid was using this particular word to describe the valiant law enforcement officer. It turned out I underestimated the man's intelligence or his sense of humor, or both. He gave us a quick assessing glance, smiled, and turned away. He must have picked up on the happy notes in my daughter's voice and must have presumed, quite correctly, that no threat to public order was coming from those quarters. The incident made me realize, however, that Lydia was not completely impervious to the change of scenery and was intensely looking for some familiar points of contact. I got irrefutable proof a few days later.

For a few days upon our arrival to Moscow, Lydia was silent and obviously thinking about something very intensely. I was curious to find out what it was, but did not want to rush things, and decided to let her thoughts come to fruition naturally. A few days later she asked me, "Why don't our people talk like us and these unfamiliar ones do?" As difficult as it was to explain to a five-year-old such notions as nations and states, it still faded in comparison with the scare she gave me when she saw that militiaman.

My personal experience of the Western world was supplemented by my mother's detailed accounts of the receptions she attended, and of the business trips she took with my father. She would tell us at length, my brother and me, all about them. Every such sortie usually had something new and noteworthy in store for her, be it a trivial detail or something much more important. She was such a great narrator, I felt I was there with her. I could just see the impeccable straight-backed servers gliding noiselessly among guests in a crowded hall of the huge house of an Indian gentleman, or the dignified English lady showing her Audubon bird guide and serving fresh strawberries in the middle of winter on a huge silver salver.

One usually had to patiently wait for the month of June to get strawberries in Moscow. Or a linen closet full, from floor to ceiling, of neatly stacked dishcloths in every imaginable pattern and color. Or a lady who would approach any group of people with the same question, "What language is spoken here?" for she could fluently converse in French, English, Spanish, and German.

It could very well be that my interest in foreign languages stems from my subconscious desire to be like that lady, who impressed my mother so much. I certainly have a soft spot for kitchen towels, and I am still looking for a beautiful silver serving dish.

And yet, despite this head start, I was still not fully interacting with my environment. I was not part of it. My life was supposed to be in Russia, on

Russian turf, played by Russian rules. We were on a tether, of sorts. It reminded me of the pictures of trips to outer space, the astronauts securely fastened to the spaceship. I was able to observe and make short excursions into that world, but I did not really blend in. The Iron Curtain, from where I stood, apart from being partially eroded, looked rather like a glass wall with the shades slightly open, but it was still very much a wall. As a result, I did not know the inner workings of the country I was living in.

Things changed almost overnight. The US and young Russia were now part of one world. The relations between the two countries would range the whole gamut in the years to come, from Cold War to hot love to the morning after, but still, it felt as though a real wall fell. Now we were smack in the middle of an open ocean after a sheltered bay, without any safety net. For the first time in my life my course was not chartered. It was free-sailing now.

Before the dissolution of the Soviet Union, we used to be part of a social circle that was very close to the Soviet elite. Our daughters were the granddaughters of a diplomat and of a university professor. We had status and we had connections. And, with the rigidity of the Soviet system making it very hard to lose one's regalia, we had a very good chance at a fulfilling and prosperous life, by Soviet standards. There was a set of tracks laid in front of us. The girls would probably have graduated from MGIMO, married their fellow college students, and the circle of life in its local variation would have continued.

The tectonic shifts at home made us lose much of our clout, relatively, if not absolutely. It was not like we moved down some steps on the social ladder. It was more as if the invisible until that moment retractable part of it was suddenly thrust forward, toward new heights. The Russian economic and social structure changed dramatically, bringing forth a new upper crust from its depths. The country we knew and had been part of ceased to exist. The new Russia was pretty much an unfamiliar territory now as well, even more so because we were living in the States and had limited contact with family and Russian friends.

**

We were neatly dethroned in absentia, but I have always been an optimist. Revolutions are notorious for treating human life and human property without much respect. We were not decapitated and not expropriated, as history has all too many examples of, so mostly we were fine. Besides, the wind of life deposited us in one of the most developed countries in the world.

We were not the poor, tired masses entering the United States, we were well fed and well educated, but still, it was a period of great anxiety, insecurity, not knowing what to expect. The paradigm had changed. The free world was gushing at us with myriads of offers. We had many options all of a sudden, and the freedom to take them. The choice of education for our children took on a whole new perspective. What path to adopt? I do not recall asking for a particularly challenging riddle, but if I did, my prayers were certainly answered.

I had to put my "grey cells" to work. Day and night, the same thought resonated in my head, the staccato of its sharp words tapping against my brain with frenetic urgency, like stilettos on the pavement or raindrops against the window. What to do, what to do? I did not want to be destroyed by this social cataclysm as rigid structures are destroyed in an earthquake. I did not want to crumble with the old regime. I had to adopt myself to the new reality, first of all, to the new level of freedom. I did not want to fall prey to the dangers of the sudden exposure to it. Freedom is a powerful force that can be treacherous, as every other force, be it natural or social. You can either learn to understand it and ride it, like a surfing wave, to go a long way, or it can kill you. I remembered my skiing accident only too well. So, I had to learn to become an educated consumer, as the Syms' slogan went, to learn to discriminate, to redefine our needs, and readjust our goals. In other words, to come up with yet another strategy.

I was not used to making my own choices. The state monopoly on the means of production in the Soviet Union meant we did not have to choose our phone company or electricity supplier, let alone make more loaded choices. We had district hospitals to cure our ailments and district schools to teach our children. One did not have the plethora of choices that America offers, and one did not need to shop for something in the sense of choosing the right goods for the right price. The prices for identical items were the same practically all over the country, and the amount of goods available was fairly limited. There was no competition. Grocery shopping was more like a hunt back in those days, usually leaving very little room for choice. You never really knew what you might get. You may have found a makeshift stall selling oranges, but it also could very well be a stall selling bananas or mushrooms. The modus operandi was more like "take whatever comes your way."

As it were, I resembled a poor person who had won the lottery, all of a sudden coming into possession of a huge amount of money. It is so much better to be introduced gradually to new opportunities and also to learn some self-discipline as a mechanism to resist self-destructive temptations along the arduous way to the top.

Those must have been truly difficult times, for Lydia apparently had sensed that tension. Once, when she was almost twelve years old, she all of a sudden burst into tears. Fearing some major problem I asked her what the matter was. In the few seconds it took her to answer, I went through dozens of potential possibilities. She was absolutely happy a few minutes ago. What could have happened? Who could have upset her that much? A boy, a friend, a teacher? When she finally calmed down enough to blurt out the answer, it was the last thing I expected to hear. "How am I going to know what medical insurance plan to choose when I grow up?" she cried.

The issue of choice can be truly overwhelming, and you certainly have to learn to quickly adjust to the ever-changing reality. When the girls were very young, before school, Alex and I would occasionally give them a nickel or dime to run to our local candy store and get some candy. They would usually buy their favorite, Bazooka chewing gum. They liked to blow bubbles. Eventually, we started to give them a dollar each to buy a little snack after school. Obviously, they were thrilled to get such an amazing treasure the first time we gave them their dollars. Alex and I let them go into the store by themselves and waited outside. Less than a minute later, they came out with brown bags full of candy, smiling from ear to ear. Each bag had twenty Bazookas. They were eight and five years old, respectively, but still, I was a little disappointed that they did not look beyond the familiar and did not use their dollars to explore new possibilities that had previously not been available to them.

Alex was working in the UN when the Soviet Union fell, in the field of economics, doing exactly what he was trained and loved to do. It was a considerable and secure source of income, but going back to Russia to try and take advantage of the many opportunities that opened up, as it is always the case at times of great upheaval, hoping to make a quick fortune was of course very tempting. It was a time when drastic career moves were in fashion, with various outcomes, both successful and not so successful. Having just watched the movie, *Protocol*, conveniently released just a few years before the turmoil and which duly refreshed my memory of the issues so well described by O. Henry, I was keen not to get duped based on the lack of experience living in a new environment, and because sometimes we tend to want to get something for nothing.

We had two young children. I was not in favor of taking risks, especially ones that were not well founded. I thought the odds were not in our favor. We were not there when the new forces were simmering in the depth of Russia, getting ready to boil over. We did not know them and we were not a part of them. The momentum was pretty much lost. I preferred to tread cautiously, to avoid rocking the boat.

Mostly, though, I coveted another thought that was keeping me from wanting to experiment and made me prefer to stay put. My new strategy was slowly taking shape. Along with most parents, I felt very strongly that our goal, as parents, was to give our children the best education possible. With Russia now becoming part of the world community, the best and most prestigious Russian higher education institutions would not be enough. Besides, as was already evident, the dissolution of the Soviet Union would inevitably lead to the collapse of the Soviet educational system. It was apparent that before long it would be in shambles, and it would take some time for the new system, meeting the new requirements, to emerge.

From the point of view of our daughters' education then, it made no sense to go back. Already, the integration process made western education a very hot commodity in Russia. I realized that in a few short years, the most successful Russian businessmen would send their children to study abroad. Europe was less expensive as far as education went, yet, along with millions of others, I thought that if one could make it in America, one could make it anywhere.

There was no doubt in my mind that solid American colleges and universities gave the widest potential opportunities to their graduates. We were already "where the puck was going to be," to employ yet again the overused words by Wayne Gretzky. Our children could be educated at one of those institutions. This became my goal for the ten years to come. UNIS, being an international school, would serve as an intermediary step between us and the new realities and give us additional time to readjust.

In the meantime, I still felt like the way I imagine Dorothy to have felt after waking up in a totally unfamiliar place following the big tornado. To regain my bearings, I had to open the doors wide, get out and follow the yellow brick road. But first, I had to find it.

Chapter Sixteen

I looked around with new eyes. Very much like Dorothy, there was one thing I was pretty sure of right away. It was not Kansas, or rather, it was not the Soviet Union. Also, I was not somewhere quiet and peaceful. To stick to the road analogies, I had to find my path not among country roads with an occasional tractor or truck, but in New York, on a five-lane expressway with eighteen-wheelers with their drag and slick Jaguars and Porsches zipping by. Once again, a great case study!

I would have to be a trailblazer, of sorts, as we were the first of a kind, at least within our limited circle. I felt like an explorer navigating unchartered waters or a lonely pioneer pushing his wagon further and further West, having but a faint idea of what lay ahead. I was back to having a lot of catching up to do. I did not want to wing it and rely solely on the school and just make sure our girls got good grades. I had to be at least one step ahead of them in order to be able to help and guide them.

I had to learn the rules of a completely new game. I had to learn how this huge and so very diverse country lived, what made it successful, what made it tick. I had to get to the core of the American system, to understand the best I could its true mechanics. My goal was to integrate our children into this world and raise them to be as happy and successful in it as possible. I did not want our daughters to live on the outskirts, figuratively speaking, in the still backwaters. I wanted them to thrive on that five-lane highway. My affinity to quotes and maxims must have become all but very apparent by now. They are like the labels on volumes of human dealings to me, their succinct summaries. The guiding principle I adopted in my mind was "the sky is the limit," which was more or less the first expression I picked up when I started to learn about our new home. It remains my favorite.

I realized that if I wanted to help our children succeed in America, the person who needed an education first of all was me. Our world is decidedly full of paradoxes. To educate someone else, one has to constantly keep learning.

The next time I went outside with my children, I picked up a copy of *Time* magazine, one of the first issues we received since Alex had subscribed to it. Since those days, it has been more than a magazine to me. It is an old friend who helps guide me and has never failed me. I had dozens of dog-eared copies with underlined words I would look up in a huge tome of the English-Russian dictionary after lunch, during my official self-education time of the day. The convenience of the online version of Merriam-Webster I use nowadays was not yet available.

I was fluent in English by that time, still, familiar routine followed—ten new words a day until I could not come up with ten new words in a reasonable amount of time and dropped it to five, and later, to two. I also started to master the computer, with the same rigorous obstinacy. One hour after lunch was dedicated to reading instructions for Windows (it was the 3.1 version when I started), Word Perfect, and ultimately Word and Excel, and to testing my newly acquired skills on our computer. I started reading *PC Magazine* to remain current. I did not watch TV or read a book for fun until late in the evening. In those years, however, practically everything I read or learned otherwise was analyzed through the lens of usability in the child-rearing process. I was learning for them, and because of them. I was educating myself in order to educate them.

I continued reading *The New York Times*. I wanted to know what books the Americans read and wrote, what movies they liked, what art moved them, and most importantly, why. And of course, I read everything I could find on child-rearing and education in America.

In the beginning, I would do homework with our children, going through every assignment. I had to figure out what was expected of them. I wanted to know what values were instilled by American books and by American TV, so I read their books and I watched TV with them. I allowed the girls to watch two hours of TV daily and let them choose their own shows. They continued with their music lessons. I still kept the practice time at one hour a day.

Very soon after the collapse of the Soviet Union, a very pertinent and difficult question arose. There was a strong sense that we were part of one world now. After so many years of confrontation, the stress was now on this oneness, and not on the cultural differences. Still, how much of their Russian heritage did I want to pass on to our girls and how?

Not unlike the ecological release in nature, cultural differences may create an advantage. Or not. When going on a long journey, you must pack only the most necessary, the most precious of your possessions. I believe that one's roots are one of these prized possessions. Strong roots make any tree stronger. But the Soviet mentality, as incompatible with the American way, and now the way of the new Russia, and thus potentially detrimental, had to go. As I saw it, one of the principles of the Soviet economic system was often to push the weak forward at the expense of the strong. The American way was to promote the strong but have a safety net to catch those that needed it. I made a painful decision to limit the girls' exposure to the books and films of the Soviet era, although there were many masterpieces among them. I did not want the Soviet mentality to infiltrate their still malleable minds. I had to do this triage, this sorting for them, find the common denominator of the human cultural heritage.

On a practical note, I wanted our daughters to be bilingual and enjoy the enormous richness of the Russian culture. It is both extremely diverse and beautiful. Russia has given the world hundreds of writers, composers, painters, singers, musicians, and dancers. I made sure our children were exposed to their works.

I tried to give them the best of their cultural heritage. We studied Russian every evening. I dropped all the other subjects of the Russian school curriculum, except for the Russian language and Russian literature. For ten years—the length of secondary education in Russia at that time—we wrote Russian dictations and did other exercises. We did every one of them from the Russian schoolbooks that I would buy every year in Moscow. I read to our girls all the Russian classics suggested by the Russian school program, the last book before they left for college being *Anna Karenina*. A third language was offered in UNIS in the seventh grade, and usually students chose their mother tongue. We opted for Spanish instead, and continued with our Russian studies at home. My school gold medal came in handy. I usually had no problems navigating the notorious complexities of the Russian orthography and syntax.

A rather detailed plan was thus put into place and I proceeded in earnest with its realization. There was just one caveat. I had to give up the idea of any career for myself, at least in the traditional sense. I was aware that this had to become the point of no return in my life. "Always think of what will happen next," my father liked to say. On the verge of the most significant decision in my life, I was doing just that.

Soviet degrees were not valid in the United States. The only place that accepted them was the UN. While being the wife of a Soviet employee, I could not get a professional position in the UN. After the collapse of the Soviet Union, I still couldn't, but for a different reason. The Russian monetary contribution to the UN became very small compared to the number of Russian employees then working at the UN. Russia became an overrepresented country. A freeze on new recruitment of Russians followed.

The other option was, of course, to get a new degree from an American college. It meant, in practical terms, time and money taken from the kids's education. Money was a less serious consideration for me at that point. I could have gone to a city or state university. Time, however, was another factor. I had to be realistic. To investigate potential career paths, to study to earn the degree, and to set my career in motion would have required a huge time commitment. Was it tempting to try my hand when there was no cap on my own career in the world where the sky was the limit? It was, very much so. But I knew perfectly well that I was no Super Woman. No claim to fame here. I was sure I would not be able to handle both our children's education and my own career.

My personal happiness and the understanding of my mission in life hinged on their success, however, not mine. Our family was at a turning point, our generation was a crucial link in determining its future destiny. I did not want to jeopardize this future. Sometimes I could be very sensible. I knew I could not do everything I wanted to do in this life, but I decided to try to go for the most important thing. One of the biggest favors we can do for ourselves in life is to set realistic goals. It is a very effective trick to be successful.

However, this was also one of the most difficult things to do. Specifically, not to play it safe or be overly ambitious, to find the perfect fit. Otherwise I felt my strategy would be like a piece of clothing two or three sizes smaller than my actual size, bought on a huge sale in hopes of going on a strict diet, and hanging uselessly in the closet from that day on, only to wind up in the pile for charity in a couple of years without being worn once.

When in due time I started to research the completely unfamiliar concept of standardized tests, one of the recommended techniques reminded me of my situation. Students taking prep courses are told not to waste time on a difficult question. If they don't know the answer, they are told to just skip the question and go to the next one, and come back to it later only if they have some time left. I did just that. I skipped one generation. I had no time to waste. Or maybe I should say, no time to squander. "Squander" was the first SAT word Lydia and Nathalie learned when they started to prepare for the test in the seventh grade, when I had them do their own version of ten new words a day.

The first time I faced a choice between career and family was when our older daughter was about to be born and I did not even realize I had a choice, but this time I was going into it with my eyes wide open. It was a strategic move, with all the risks assessed as best I could.

At a critical bend of the road, I wanted my life to be part of a bigger scheme and streamlined to the maximum, for me to be able to give the next generation a much needed boost. I was not looking to carve a niche for myself. Rather, I saw myself as part of a continuum. My goals did not start and end with me.

Remembering one's mortality makes one enjoy life to the fullest, take advantage of every moment of it. On the other hand, we should remain humble. Memento mori, indeed.

The true meaning and the true beauty of a human life, in a way, is to forget about death. One will not be able to soar very high if one keeps thinking about the inevitable eventual landing.

If we change the point of reference, do not take death into account, and set our goals beyond the limits of our own life, look at ourselves as part of a bigger unit, the perspective is certainly different. There is a better chance our life will not contradict the general pattern then and will not be crushed, like a car that goes against traffic. Maybe this is exactly what "to know yourself" means: to find where your piece of the puzzle goes. It does not mean to conform or to pretend. It means to find your true nature, your place in the grand scheme of life and make some part of you, by the same token, immortal.

Was I so absolutely certain our children needed my help? Not at all. I did not know the odds, and I did not want to take any chances, but this was only partially the reason. I would say it was its rational component, the workings of my philosophizing, scrutinizing mind. It just felt like a smart thing to do. My head, however, usually lags behind my heart. This was just a rational explanation of my initial impulse. Usually, if not always, my brain would conveniently churn out the appropriate explanation after the deed. I have always felt first, and known later.

Our children were at a clear disadvantage. They would have had to start not just from zero, but from a negative value. Other kids had parents they could turn to for advice, for guidance, for help. I wanted our girls to have that, too., Although I was not at all sure I could help to begin with. I couldn't not try. I could not let them go into this difficult struggle all alone. It felt like throwing our daughters into life they knew nothing about and hoping the right instincts would kick in.

Many years later, in Mexico with my husband and kids, we took part in the release of baby sea turtles, just hatched the previous day, into the wild. It was dusk. We were each given a small container with a little black creature, two or three inches long. When prompted, we simultaneously put them on the sand. Without as much as a second-long hesitation, the tiny reptiles headed toward the ocean, plunging fearlessly into the dark waves. I couldn't help feeling scared for them, but at the same time in awe witnessing this powerful instinct. Looking at those baby turtles, I remembered my feelings of long ago.

I guess, come to think of it, to leave our girls to their own devices felt at the end of the day, not only shortsighted, but also immoral. Now I have started to think that, in the grand scheme of life, what is immoral is usually not smart. I certainly did not think along those lines back then, however. It just seemed heartless and I could not do it. Long before I read *The Divine Comedy* and got Dante's take on the hierarchy of human sins, I just could not do what felt to me as an act of utmost betrayal and cruelty.

It was a question of preserving my integrity, not a sacrifice. My genes must be a particularly selfish breed. I have never felt any demarcation line between me and my children. I *am* my children.

Our children have never been separate entities to me. Their success has always been my success, but not in the sense of living vicariously through them. As tempting as it might have been, I never tried to extend my life by robbing our kids of theirs and trying to make them achieve my goals. To me, being told how to live has always felt like copying someone else's homework. The most exciting thing to me has always been to solve the puzzle myself, not just look up the answers on the next page or at the end of the book. I did not want our children to suffer from what I knew I would suffer from. So I have never tried to snatch up their lives. I gave them mine.

As I write this, I pause. While I did have those thoughts and those feelings at the time, still, I have the disturbing sensation that it just does not explain everything. My decision was made much earlier, years before the Soviet Union collapsed and even before our children were born.

***

My school was right across from our apartment building, and I had been walking there alone since the first grade. School started at 8:30 in the morning, and it was still pitch-dark outside when I left home during the long Russian winter months. I remember how reluctant I was to get out of my warm bed in the feverish yellow light of my table lamp and go into that cold dark night. Once outside, however, I did not mind it anymore. I left a little earlier to make sure I would be on time, and our courtyard was usually deserted and absolutely silent. The air was young and fresh, the snow gleaming and creaking merrily under my feet. It was the very beginning of a new day, and during the few short minutes of my walk it felt as though it was all mine.

We were released from school at around noon in those years. I would rush home and try to finish my homework before my lunchtime at one o'clock. My lunch and eventually our family's dinner was something my mother would spend a good part of her morning cooking from scratch every day. It consisted of hot soup, an entrée, and a dessert. Feeling nice and warm from my meal, I would go outside to play with my friends. I loved those hours the most, and was invariably the last man—last girl, rather—

standing. After the last kid had gone home to do his or her homework, I would hang in there for a few more minutes, slide a few more times from the little ice mountain on my sled, and desperately bored, already at dusk, would head for home at last.

One such afternoon, when the cold was especially bitter, I sneaked into our school with a gang of my friends. At the far end of the hallway, I saw a few kids going noiselessly and purposefully about their business. Those were children enrolled in a so-called prolonged-day program, which meant they stayed in school after classes and were picked up by their parents on their way home after work. The school building was well heated, but I felt chilly and uneasy all of a sudden.

On many occasions in later years, I heard that the Moscow sky is often grey and overcast. I was very surprised to hear it. It turned out to be true. I checked. I did not remember it to be. Our house was always sunny and warm with the steady tender glow of my mother's love.

I left school and went straight home. I did not feel like hanging out that day. I wanted to stay in the sun. The rest is pure mathematics.

By the time our girls had started school I had already practically come to terms with the idea of having to give up my postgraduate degree. One fine day shortly after my aborted attempt at writing at the skating rink, I got a package from my father. It turned out that he had written my thesis for me. My father had no background in economics. The paper was not great, but it was perfectly defendable. I was not interested in a bogus degree, but after getting such a reminder and such a boost, I started to work seriously on my paper. Time, ever so precious. I started to wake up at six every morning and go to bed at midnight, sometimes later, if I was on a lucky streak and ideas kept pouring in. By the end of that year I had my thesis. I do not think it was stellar, but it had the honest advantage of being mine, and I truly liked the main ideas. Not being very robust, I guess, I also got vicious headaches that would only ease their grip on me a few years later.

The way things worked out, by the time I was about to finalize my work, I was in Russia alone with the girls for a few months already. We were outside once, heading to our favorite toy store. In front of us, two kids were trotting happily with their father. "Lucky them," said Nathalie. "They have a father!"

Helen Trepelkov

In about two weeks, we were on a plane to New York. And that was the end of my one and only youthful escapade, my unfortunate flirtation with a scientific career. Soon the Soviet Union fell, and the way I saw it, the idea of defending my thesis became obsolete. When time is at a premium, you have to cut out unnecessary motions. I already did the most important thing for me—I had finished writing it and it had been approved for defense. The rest would have been a luxury I could not afford, under the circumstances. I regarded staying another four to five months in Moscow to get the actual PhD as a selfish act of self-promotion without any practical value in the US. But it did not come easy. I did regret it, and the thought caused me pain for a long time. To look on the bright side, I never had the middle-age crisis. I had all my crises back then, in my youth, and was done with them.

I realized the potential dangers of being a stay-at-home mom, notably being a wife without an income, fully dependent on my husband. Soviet moral code, especially the rules imposed on its Foreign Service corps, did not encourage divorce. With the collapse of the Soviet Union, however, so did its moral rules and restrictions. Now our family lives were our own. People do fall in and out of love, and we were still very young at the time. One has to be realistic and honest. I did not hedge my bets. I was taking a risk, and I was fully aware of it on a rational level. But somehow I have never believed it in my heart. Besides, I don't believe in hedging my bets in personal matters. I noticed that people who do take precautions turn out to need them the most, at the end of the day. I prefer Napoleon Bonaparte's tactics. First engage in a serious battle and then see what happens.

There was another issue, too. If I achieved my goal and our children became successful, they may look at me in many years as a complete failure. I was testing myself again. Stakes were higher this time. A few condescending looks of my peers would be nothing compared to the contempt of my own children. What if the girls were to grow up and tell me, "You have done nothing with your life." It was a chilling thought. I preferred not to dwell on it, but I was ready to face the consequences. The answer came quickly and easily. If it came to that, that would only mean that I did not do my job well, and essentially, I would deserve it. But if I could manage for the girls to be successful and still respect me, then I would have succeeded. It would mean that they did not compromise, in their turn, did not settle, but went for what they loved, because only then would they be able to understand, to accept, and to approve of me. It felt like I was betting it all, hoping to hit the jackpot. But then again, is life worth living for anything less?

I realized that my input could be, at best, that of a little tugboat that leads beautiful ocean liners from the shallow mooring waters out into the open sea and usually is not given much thought or credit. I knew that this time, there would be no way I could catch up, no way I could ever go along. So be it, as long as there were beautiful ocean liners.

I could never really accept the thought that I would have to stay ashore, however. I do believe that mothers have an uncanny power to follow their children wherever they go and remain their guardians. Because you don't really have to understand your children. You have to trust them, to believe in them, and to forgive them.

I was about to start a long journey. I set out to construct a new building according to a new and unfamiliar design. I was on a quest for new building blocks, the building blocks of my own American dream. I had to deconstruct the reality to its original primary units and take those that seemed fit for my purpose. The new twist on my task seemed hugely ambitious and sometimes overwhelming, but also very worthy and just plain right. I was happy and at peace with myself.

Chapter Seventeen

All that was very nice thinking indeed, but it was much easier said than done. Where would I begin?

The logical starting point would be, it seemed, to do as the Romans do, when in Rome. I heard this saying a lot while growing up. For many years, it was quietly stashed somewhere in the back of my memory, just waiting for the right moment to pop out. At the time, it meant mostly that I had to respect the rules of the hosts when we were visiting our numerous friends and relatives. Now the saying acquired a new connotation, if not a totally new meaning.

Lydia's birthday was coming up and I decided to throw her a party. No better time than now. I had to start somewhere. The vestiges of the iron wall were still there. It was not recommended for Soviet people to socialize with foreigners, so I had very little practical knowledge about how such parties were organized in America. We lived very modestly, words like "home design" could hardly apply, which presented an additional challenge.

I was working on the party day and night, trying to take into consideration every possible detail. Still, it was a very simple party. We had no professional entertainers. I had no idea such a thing even existed at the time. The main draw was games with prizes, and the main entertainer was me. The children were very excited to win colorful pens, pencils, and other little favors. Late into the night before the party, I was taping balloons to the ceiling of our living room. I spaced them one yard apart and it looked to me, unaccustomed as I was to lavish living, very festive. When by the end of the party we were out of games, but the gang was thirsty for more prizes, these balloons saved the day. I proclaimed the final challenge was to try to get a balloon from the ceiling. It became the highlight of the party. It caused me some trouble with our downstairs neighbors, too. The stomping and the jumping were considerable. When the kids were leaving, I heard one boy say to his mother, enthusiastically, "This was the best party, Mom." These words, uttered by a small boy, marked my right of passage. From that moment on, I believed I could do it.

***

The most salient element and the first thing one notices is, of course, clothes. There is more to it than meets the eye, however. Clothes do not make the man, but they can certainly make a girl miserable. My own experiences as far as clothes were concerned, were varied and many. I was cherry-picking those that seemed relevant.

I wore a uniform in the Russian school, as was the custom those days in the Soviet Union, but there were no such requirements in the Swiss school. If I was an exotic bird there, it was certainly not by my plumage. I had just two or three very basic outfits. I thought I saw satisfaction and pleasure on the face of my class teacher when I finally got a stylish new outfit at some point during the eighth grade. I was fourteen. I did not ask my parents for more clothes. Mostly because at that time, they thought I was too young to be interested in such things as clothes and were absolutely unaware that that was not the case. So I was embarrassed to point out their negligence.

In general, I did not like to ask for anything because I knew they were doing what they could as it was. The remuneration of Soviet people abroad was structured so as to closely match the conditions at home. We did not have to pay any rent or our medical expenses, but we did not have a lot of free cash. We could not afford to buy many things and to maintain an active lifestyle as well. My parents valued experience over material things way before this philosophy became the latest trend. Shopping was not their forte. They did not shop, per se. They would go to a store only when they could not avoid it.

They preferred to travel and to take us places. And I liked our life. I liked our travels around the country and all over Europe, wandering through world-renowned museums and cathedrals, walking the same streets that Leonardo da Vinci and Michelangelo must have walked, or retracing the steps of Napoleon before his last battle. I also liked our quieter weekends, with my father rowing the boat on some peaceful mountain lake, having hot chocolate with pastries or enjoying my favorite ice cream dessert, *a coupe maison*, in some random quaint town. Or our winter skiing and skating in the mountains, with an obligatory snowmobile ride and a cheese fondue afterward. Or just seeing a Disney movie on a Sunday night. My parents had my tacit approval.

Still, I was aware of the problem and annoyed by it. I was not particularly bothered or injured simply because I did not compete, did not mesh with other students. I was part of a totally different world, so my ego did not suffer in the least. I am not sure I would have been so carefree had I been considered not well-dressed by Soviet standards. That was what mattered back then. The most coveted thing was, of course, the blue jeans. Here is one of the Russian jokes of those days, to give you an idea of what it meant to have jeans in the Soviet Union in the seventies of the last century: A man with means goes to see a dentist. It turns out he needs his tooth capped. "Should I use gold or porcelain?" the dentist asks. "None of those cheapos," the man replies. "Use blue jeans."

I had two pairs, so I really had my bases covered.

The fact remains, I had firsthand experience with the awkwardness standing out can cause, and I did not want our girls to experience it. My immediate response was pretty simple. Life is tough enough, we should not inflict unwarranted pain if we can avoid it.

It is not very smart either. The pressure builds up, and if thwarted, could lead to an outburst sooner or later. It is better to control the when and the how than to leave it to chance, which may lead to a serious case of revolt at a most inappropriate moment. Even if the wish seemed stupid, I felt kids should outgrow it themselves.

My patience was put to test repeatedly during those years. Nathalie's aesthetic sense caused me considerable pain on more than a few occasions when she was young. I do not claim that mine is flawless, but that we certainly did not see eye to eye as far as style was concerned when she was a child. It all started when Nathalie was five and insisted on wearing a baby blue sportive windbreaker with a bohemian-style patchwork skirt in burgundy hues. I winced every time I looked at this ensemble. I did not appreciate its eclectic nature or the color scheme. I enjoyed it so much when our girls looked pretty and neat. I ironed their small fine cotton blouses when they were preschoolers, even while we were living in our country house. I let Nathalie have her way, nonetheless.

When she was in the second grade, she shocked my senses again by asking for red Reebok sneakers. That was a daring move to begin with. They did not exactly match the rest of her wardrobe. To make things worse, she particularly liked to wear them with a turquoise tank top and a full turquoise skirt with black polka dots. I almost fainted just looking at this jarring combination, but again, I let her buy and wear those sneakers. I was absolutely certain that I was the one who should suck it up, not Nathalie. She was not ready to understand had I tried to explain. I wanted her to experiment on her own. If she wanted my advice, I was always there. Her favorite color is gray now, by the way, not that I had anything to do with that evolution either.

I was not in the way. I did not want to constrict the girls unless there was a particular need to do so. I was never in a hurry to say no. Moreover, when I got too excited and moved too much to the beat of my own drum, I backed up. When Lydia was turning eleven, I went on a shopping spree and bought her three or four outfits that I found very pretty. They were fluffy, girly affairs with white and pink prominently present. I wrapped everything nicely and put all the boxes on her nightstand after she had already fallen asleep on the eve of her birthday.

Holidays were big events in our family when I was growing up, especially birthdays. Presents were put on my bedside table late at night so I would wake up and see them first thing in the morning. I enjoyed it very much, so I did the same for our daughters.

My grandmother Olga, on the other hand, was a stalwart and had an old-fashioned approach to the holidays. She never invited or reminded anyone about her birthday. It was considered an invitation for a present, and consequently, highly improper. Instead, she would have a festive meal ready, including mounds of sweet and savory freshly baked goodies, from early morning on, to greet anybody who remembered and dropped in to wish her happy birthday.

I set my alarm for six o' clock and was impatiently waiting for Lydia to wake up. Sure enough, I heard her unwrapping her presents soon after. She obviously was very eager to see what they were. And then—nothing. I waited a little longer. Something was not right. I entered the girls' room and found Lydia quietly crying in their bathroom. She hated all the clothes I had so lovingly picked for her. And I was so proud of my choices!

Just like that, I practically missed our daughter becoming a teenager, or rather a preteen. I left the house so swiftly, I had to pace back and forth for quite some time with my huge bag in front of the store, waiting for it to open, to return everything. Eventually I bought some strange-looking overalls and other equally odd pieces of clothing I would have never perceived as beautiful without Lydia's help.

At about the same time, Lydia had her first dance. A bunch of her friends came to our house to get ready. They quickly disappeared into the girls' room, but I heard their excited whispers and giggles as they tried on clothes and put on makeup. Presently, they reappeared, all made up and dressed to the nines, bursting with satisfaction with the results of their hard work and a newly acquired sense of self-importance. It was a dazzling and dizzying spectacle. Subtlety was certainly not the main goal of their labors. I managed to squeeze out that they all looked wonderful. Then I looked at Lydia. She had on bright red lipstick. It did not match her delicate features at all. She looked at me, ready to stand her ground and yet uncertain and yearning for approval. I was speechless and just looked at her in shock. Without a word, she darted back into her room and chose a softer color.

My own first experiences with makeup dated back to the time I was studying in Switzerland, and they were pretty similar to Lydia's. We were allowed to wear it and consequently it was not an issue. When at 15 I started the ninth grade in Russia, on the other hand, girls were not allowed to wear as much as face powder even in high school, let alone at a younger age. There were also very strict rules as far as our hair was concerned. When I started school at seven, girls' hair still had to be braided, although by the time I graduated, other hairdos, ponytails for instance, were allowed, as long as hair remained up. The school administrators did not go after a few "lost souls," girls who were not pursuing any particular academic goals or were not very much involved in the social life of the class, but the rest complied. The misery could definitely reach Shakespearean heights when the boy you had a crush on had an unobstructed view of a pimple on your forehead exposed curtesy of your hair pulled back tightly in the aforementioned deplorable, detestable ponytail. At any rate, on such days, the sorry attempts of the teachers to draw your attention to the treasures of human knowledge were absolutely and unequivocally lost.

A few weeks after Lydia's first dance, with those memories in mind, I bought her a big chest of makeup, full of shades and lipsticks in all colors, along with other wonderful and indispensable trappings. Nathalie was never very interested, but Lydia loved to experiment and would hold makeup sessions and practice on all of her and Nathalie's friends. She soon became very good at it.

That was the time that the popularity concern started to creep into the girls' lives. Again, I was inclined to up the ante and let the girls face rather than eschew the notorious peer pressure. I wanted them to feel good about themselves. It is a natural desire to feel beautiful and confident, and I did not want to suppress or ignore it. In youth, beauty and strength rule. I did not want our girls to lose, or more importantly, get used to losing. I wanted them to be fighters. Yet, watching the coming-of-age boys and girls in the throngs of their first struggles for influence and power, I did not want our children to get carried away and lose perspective. I urged them to remember the joke they told me themselves. What will you call a nerd in twenty years? *Boss.*

I kept telling the girls not to count on good looks, for few things are more ephemeral than physical beauty, especially if pitched against dire financial conditions and life's hardships. In not so many years, an average-looking girl who may not look particularly pretty now, if she perseveres and succeeds in life, will be able to afford beautiful clothes, great skin products and makeup, and she will be able to attend the best hair salons and spas. As a result, she will probably look much better than many of the teenage beauties that used to scoff at her in school. When, exhausted by my own loquaciousness, I would finally stop lecturing, the result of my toils would be the patient polite stare of Lydia's immaculately made-up eyes. She usually got the brunt of my educational fervor as the older of the girls, while Nathalie would quietly sit and listen to my discourses from afar.

Once, when Lydia was already in high school, we went to a department store together. She liked some top that cost much more than we could afford at the time. For the umpteenth time, I told her that if she wanted to buy such things one day, she had to consider working very hard and making a lot of money. Something stirred in the depth of her eyes. I was pretty sure it finally sank in that time. Encouraged by my success, I continued to hammer this banal truth into the girls' minds. Sometime later, Lydia interrupted my all-too-familiar homily about the importance of working in earnest. Looking at me with tender fondness and just a smidgeon of condescension, yet very seriously, she told me, "You don't have to worry about me, Mom. I will always make a living. I do not mind working hard."

At one point during her college years, she called me in distress. She was just beginning her junior year of Georgetown's McDonough School of Business and was about to start working in her prospective field during the school year and not only during summers to acquire some work experience by the time she graduated from college. She had already accepted two internships by that time. Now, she was offered a third one in a very prestigious firm. She was very tempted to accept, but having three jobs would be extremely hard, and she considered it unethical to go back on her word and quit one of the first two after she had accepted the offers. I agreed with her, as she had anticipated, but I did not tell her what to do. She accepted the job, but kept the first two as well. At that point, I knew that I would not have to worry about her, indeed.

Chapter Eighteen

From early on, I did not want the girls to be lulled by the fact that when one is a child, very often a new T-shirt from the Gap or a new Nintendo game is all one needs to feel perfectly content and on top of their game. I liked to stress the fact that although the most important things in life are indeed priceless, for many others one had better have a MasterCard.

To keep it all from being entirely theoretical, I enthusiastically embraced the concept of an allowance from very early on. I was never given money on a regular basis as a child. I think that was more or less the general custom among the families around us. Neither was I provided with opportunities to earn it until I entered college and got my first college stipend. I consulted some other mothers, and Alex and I started giving our girls the same amount of money the majority of kids around them got. I liked this idea a lot. It was supposed to teach them to manage money from an early age, and also to instill other generally valuable skills, for instance, how to control their everyday urges and opt to achieve bigger goals. I remember how impressed I was when I learned that in America, math problems for young kids often involved money. No child would like to be short-changed, in the literal sense! I think it's a great down-to-earth incentive to learn arithmetic.

Mostly, I wanted our girls to know that you need money to buy things you want. From this basic principle, one is free to decide how much one is willing to work to get where one wants to be. I felt that the earlier the child realizes that this is one of the practical reasons he or she is studying and what the implications of it are, the better. We opened individual checking accounts for our girls when they started junior school. They were free to spend or deposit their allowances, partially or in their entirety. By the time they went to college, each had a nice sum in savings to use on whatever they wished.

When the girls were about to leave for college and I started to investigate the matter of allowances there, I learned that some parents gave very little money to their kids, mainly, to avoid them spending it on alcohol. I felt my educational job by that time was basically done, and that it was a moment of truth for me. I trusted our daughters to do the right thing. In general, I have always preferred to err on the side of trust, going by the "fool me once, shame on you, fool me twice, shame on me" principle. If we are always on our guard, we are certainly never deceived or disappointed, but we never get to touch another human being's soul either. In this particular instance, I felt that to give very little money was mostly detrimental. Young people have a lot of needs, they want to socialize and look nice. Not having enough money could push them toward taking odd jobs indiscriminately, while from the time management point of view it made more sense to study at that point, to learn the skills necessary to make more money later on.

***

When our daughters were in junior school, Alex and I seemed to be on the same page. We both enjoyed buying cute outfits for them and treating them in other little ways. I remember the big pomp surrounding our getting them sneakers with neon laces, lime green and hot pink, so popular at the time. It was raining cats and dogs, but we were all very excited. The girls for obvious reasons, and Alex and I because we saw how much joy it brought to the girls and because we were able to afford it.

As time went by, it became apparent that Alex favored a much stricter overall approach than I did. It almost seemed like he had grown up, transitioning seamlessly into parental mode, and I had remained a child myself. He was very much opposed to makeup and any clothes he deemed inappropriate for school, his idea of inappropriate being very broad. He liked to tell us that he started wearing a business suit his freshman year of college and had been wearing it ever since. He did not exactly stress the fact that he was not that thrilled about it at the time. I was sometimes afraid that he would like to improve on his past performance and clad our girls in some business garb starting in middle school. Alex was also very much against sleepovers and any other activities that he thought would detract from our girls' studying.

I had my first encounter with the concept of dressing for success in high school. When I was in the ninth, penultimate grade of the Soviet school, I caught pneumonia. It was, not surprisingly, during wintertime. When I was finally well enough to go back to school after more than a month of staying at home, my father went to talk to the director. He asked her to allow me to wear a wool cardigan over the uniform occasionally, when the weather was especially cold. It was January, a particularly vicious month as far as temperatures were concerned. Minus five or ten degrees Fahrenheit was pretty much the norm. The director told my father that if I wanted to consider earning a gold medal, which I did, I had to be a paragon for other students in everything, my appearance included. I wanted the gold medal and I did not care, to be frank, about the cardigan, so the idea of a cardigan was dropped. What made me suffer much more was my parents' unyielding unwillingness to let me wear western cloths to the school dances. The promise of a gold medal shone much less brightly at that point, and I had no choice but to take it in stride.

A few years later, when I was pregnant with Lydia, I learned, quite by accident, what was in all likelihood behind the suit rule imposed by Alex's and my parents' decisions as well. Our apartment was being painted, and I left the premises so as not to inhale the fumes. I went into our local candy store and picked up a magazine. It had an article about the dress code for working women. I read on. Among other suggestions, one was advised to dress according to the position one was seeking to get. I took notice then. Still, I felt that for middle school, considering UNIS did not require its students to wear a uniform, the goal of mastering American culture was ambitious enough. There was no need to skip developmental stages. Corporate culture and its attributes could wait a few more years, should the girls be so inclined as to join the ranks of its adherents.

To fit in creates a much more beneficial surrounding, promotes a much smoother integration of children into the world around them, and has a much gentler impact on their psyche. To be strong enough to differ, we first have to acquire a sense of belonging. No book should be judged by its cover, granted, but young children are not very proficient at reading yet, and they often do. When you are not like everyone else, you have to put up an additional fight, and you'd better have some additional ammunition, which children often lack. On top of that, just like future artists learn painting by first copying old masters, I felt girls had to fit in first, and then find their own style.

My reaction to Alex's Spartan aspirations was for these reasons very negative. I wanted our girls to have a full, happy life, with friends, being part of the community, not living like outcasts. I wanted them to wear the same clothes and participate in the same activities that other kids around them did. That was also the reason behind my idea to buy them Nintendo for their first Christmas after it became a hot item, but as with TV, they had time limits.

As usual, rational arguments started to seep in after a while. Being miserable from not belonging was not only unnecessary, but also a much bigger detractor from studying. Besides, we do not live in a vacuum. We need to interact with other people. Social activities, among other things, help children learn how to defend their views and values to achieve their goals. It is an invaluable part of education. Ultimately, people will be the judges of our work. Having academic knowledge is not enough. It is important to know how to drive your point across and how to make other people accept and respect you and whatever product you have to offer. I have always found learning about life as important as getting good grades. Also, I thought that one should have free time left to enjoy it. If you have to study all the time, you have just set your bar above your abilities, and you probably have to reevaluate your goals.

When I was graduating from college myself, I heard my father's friend comment on a boy who had scholastic trouble, "Why would he study? He has everything." I knew this boy. His father was a diplomat stationed abroad at the time. So, by "everything" this man probably meant he was allowed to drive his dad's car and had western LPs and western clothes. My father did not comment. I had everything a young girl could wish for, too, by the same token. My parents had dropped all their sartorial limitations by that time. It had no bearing on my studying, however. These things were never connected in my mind. At the time, these words hit me as a very incongruous statement, but when my own children became teenagers, I saw the logic behind this approach. To make the child earn what he wants instead of letting him or her get it for free lest he or she take it for granted and grow up idle and worthless. The goal was to give the child an incentive to work.

I have always liked to pick up analogies between the laws of the physical world and human society. An electron loses a lot of energy when jumping from a higher level to a lower one, closer to the nucleus, the "sun." Electrons that are in the outermost level have the most energy and are the most active. Isn't it the same with people? The question is, once the parents have made it, can the same drive be maintained in their children by artificial means only? When you do not have to survive, do you stop working at your full potential unless you are put in artificially strict narrow boundaries? I saw the merits of this approach and I agreed that this may be an efficient way, but I never believed it to be a valid motive and never had what it took to embrace it.

For quite some time, Alex tried to convince me to be stricter, or rather to act stricter, on his behalf. I could not do it. It was not that I was sure I was right and was doggedly pursuing my vision. I was always open to suggestions. There was no way I could know I was right. Again, it was unchartered waters for us. I was sure of one thing, nonetheless. I could only do what I believed in. I could not operate on step-by-step instructions for a different piece of equipment. I could only be myself, for better or worse. He wanted our daughters to unquestionably accept his authority. I wanted free spirits who would question mine.

Speaking of which, Nathalie once got an A for her history paper on the Industrial Revolution. It would have been just another A, if not for the fact that in that paper, she contended that the Industrial Revolution did not take place or rather, that every century contains its own Industrial Revolution, presenting a string of logical arguments in support of her ideas. The ulterior validity of her arguments notwithstanding, and my disagreement with them, I applauded the independence of her thinking. So did the teacher, who not only gave her the highest grade, but praised her profusely during the parent-teacher conference.

Difficulties do make us stronger, granted. If they don't break or kill us, that is. I guess the line between education and cruelty is a very fine and subjective one. To me, to subject our children to artificial hardships felt like betrayal. Whether they had what it took to get to the top or not was actually irrelevant. I knew I would not be able to quietly look upon them in their misery. Remember the bonsai tree disaster? Besides, there is only so much that can be achieved in one lifetime. So this perpetual beginning at the same emotional zero mark over and over, the same survival mode for every generation to come, felt like Sisyphean toil, in other words, again, like a huge waste. There had to be another way.

Alex and I had irreconcilable differences. We agreed to disagree. Alex accepted the validity of my reasoning on my need to implement my own ideas, and gave me the reins for good. I wound up with full responsibility for our girls' upbringing. I was not particularly looking for responsibility, but I was not afraid of it when it came my way. Still, I often felt uneasy, unsure that I was doing the right thing, on the verge of wavering a few times. Many a night, I would sneak out of my bed, careful not to wake Alex, and sleepless, go lie on the living room couch, thinking over my decisions. All over again, I felt lonely and needed some reassurance very badly.

It was not a riddle, it was not a play or a rehearsal. It was as serious as it could get. Our children's future was at stake. I was trying to have a peek at that future to make sure I did everything I could and chose wisely.

Besides raking my memory for some relevant incidents from my own life, I was trying to recruit supporters for my cause in the books I read. It is believed that everyone must read just three hundred books in their lifetime, but to find the right ones you have to read thousands of them. What a pleasure it is to stumble upon such a jewel of a book, to have this flicker of recognition, to realize that you, too, had the same thought, the same feeling. It is hard to overestimate the joy and relief I experienced when I found those random confirmations of my being on the right track. I was no longer lost and alone, doubting myself. It is as if, after getting lost in a forest on a hiking trip and having wandered clueless for many hours, all of a sudden you see a trail marker, and this joyful speck of paint makes you realize you were going in the right direction after all. This feeling of relief brings about a tremendous boost of energy, all of a sudden you are not tired anymore, and you feel like you can walk for many more miles.

I must have been truly desperate, for as appalling as it may seem, it was Sun Tzu and his *Art of War* that I dragged in as my major ally. "So it is said that if you know others and know yourself, you will not be imperiled in a hundred battles." I liked the odds.

So I wanted early and true engagement. I was not a fan of keeping the children from getting their driver's license, figuratively speaking. They would have to hit the road sooner or later. Wouldn't it make more sense to put your kid at the wheel, sit next, and teach her or him how to drive, first in the quiet familiar back streets, getting closer and closer to the crowded fast lane?

It is much more productive not to engage in a power struggle with our kids, but to make children feel we are on the same side of the barricades, that we will protect them until they are ready to leave the parental nest, and to learn the restrictions of life, rather than shave against artificial parental ones. I was never tough with our girls. Life is, however, and I wanted to give them strength to deal with it. Strength coming from security, not hardship. Love and support make our children grow wings.

It is certainly true that children do not choose their parents. But it is equally true, in my opinion, that children may or may not choose their parents as their mentors. I did choose mine. I feel that in order to be a good and successful teacher, children have to accept you as such. I did not only love my parents, I adhered to their values. It allowed me to take full advantage of what I was offered. It made their raising me simpler and my childhood years more productive and happier than they could have been had I been in opposition to them.

The lack of communication, small and insignificant at first, may ultimately lead to the irreversible alienation of children from their parents, instead of bringing them closer together. Parents and their children are connected as if by a set of gears. I thought that this union not only makes children stronger, but as long as such a connection exists, there exists a way to deliver ideas to the child. Children should not feel any antagonism between them and their parents. They should feel a united front against external adversity.

One cannot learn to live in the world by avoiding exposure to it. I did not mind if our girls were a little hurt in the process. When one is young, the mistakes are usually small, but the lessons are big. Some activities may feel like a waste of time or even harmful, but this is also great training. What would happen to the overprotected child without any skills to handle social interactions with his or her peers, say, in college? The child has to be exposed to potential dangers while it is still possible to manage them. I believed in gradual, reasonable risks. Step by step, we have to prepare our kids to resist temptation, to make the right choices, to deal with crises.

Besides, if children unquestionably accept our supremacy, our absolute leadership, they may later unquestionably accept the leadership of somebody else as a result. If we push children too hard and tell them what to do for too long, chances are they may be tempted to take the path of least resistance, become passive, and have no initiative or desires of their own. There is a threat to create a perfect instrument for somebody else to extract a melody.

When I was still a preschooler, my father told me once how dogs are taught to swim. Little puppies are simply thrown into the water, he told me, and they are supposed to start working their paws, which most of them start doing... I don't remember how this conversation started and what provoked it. I never had pets and never wanted or asked for one. This is rather peculiar considering both my parents had had various pets throughout their childhood. My father's faithful dog even protected him once when he ran away from home and fell asleep, exhausted by the perturbations of the day, a few hundred yards away from his house. He was four years old and did not see eye to eye with his mother in a particularly forceful manner and was punished for it, which he perceived as a great injustice on her part.

Maybe our peripatetic lifestyle was at the root of it. Whatever it was, this little piece of knowledge conveyed very seriously and in great detail remained with me, particularly because visualization was always part of my processing of the spoken or written word.

Controlled swimming was my answer. I let our girls test the waters, explore their own boundaries, and hone their personalities in the meantime. It seemed risky. It also seemed like the only way to approach the issue. Anything else would have been accepting defeat before the fight.

When I was growing up, I liked to listen to everything that was said around me. My parents even used to joke that it seemed I was fully concentrated on my building blocks or some other game, but as it turned out later, I had not missed a single word of their conversation. One of the stories I remembered was about Anastasia's older son who seemed to be obsessed by a hot kettle and would try to take it from the stove at every opportunity. He just would not listen to his mother, and no matter how many times he was told not to do it, for he would scald himself, every morning his little hand would reach for the fascinating shiny object. Exasperated, his father, a neurologist, finally told his wife to fill the kettle with water hot enough to scare the child, but not hot enough to hurt him, and let him reach it. The boy grabbed the kettle and poured all its contents on himself. He was shaken, but just enough to make him lose interest in playing with the kettle.

It seemed to me like a sound way to teach certain truths. Some things have to be lived to be understood. I wanted our daughters to experience life firsthand. I wanted to teach them to gradually take responsibility for their actions, to teach them to think, not to be the passive recipients of processed mental food. In a way, I wanted them to participate in their own upbringing. I never claimed I knew better. Choosing between the authority of power and the power of authority, I have always leaned toward the latter. I was always trying to reason with them, to make them understand and agree, and I allowed them to make their own decisions in matters that I deemed within their grasp. When one bears full responsibility for the action, one is usually trying really hard to make the right choice. When one is denied something, one is usually tempted to just fight adversity. I placed high expectations on them to make the right choice.

Sometimes, however, I would almost cry knowing that one of our daughters was on the verge of making a mistake. Following that father's reasoning, I did not try to prevent certain things from happening by prohibiting them, however. I was concentrating instead on better calibrating the level of responsibility to match the level of the child's maturity. It is much easier to just say no, for a parent. To find the right amount of responsibility I could safely delegate to our daughters was anything but. Yet I was amazed myself how often, after thinking it over, our children would choose the right thing to do. Little by little, I learned to trust their good sense. It was a wonderful feeling. Trust does seem to beget responsibility.

There was a party at Nathalie's classmate's house once, when she was in the seventh or eighth grade. Nathalie did not go. She must have sensed something was off. It turned out later that there were drugs at that party. One girl got sick. There were many kids there, but apparently only one called 911. I praised Nathalie for doing the right thing. I also told her that the girl who called 911 had already passed the exam for adulthood, in my eyes. Not to participate in doubtful events is proof of good self-protection instincts and is the first step, but we cannot always avoid the unpleasant or even potentially harmful events. To have the smarts and the guts to do the right thing when everybody else was doing the wrong one seemed to me to be testimony of a level of maturity not even all adults are capable of.

Of course, I made my share of mistakes. It is hard enough to know the right thing to do, let alone to implement it. Come to think of it, I wanted to turn two carefree delicate girls into tough modern ladies, without being one myself. Indeed, those who can't do, teach. I still remember some episodes when I clearly missed the mark. I did not let Lydia go to Paris with her friend when she was twelve. I was always promoting travel as a great educational experience and as one of the biggest joys in life, but it would have been her first independent trip, and to start with international travel felt too risky. Nathalie had it easier, since my fears were already weakened by Lydia's fights for her freedom. I let her go to Seattle to see her friend at about the same age. It was not international travel, of course, but she had to change planes in St. Louis. She was supposed to arrive in Seattle close to midnight. We agreed she would call me from the airport in Seattle when she got there. She did call me from St. Louis, and then she disappeared. I started calling her cell phone—no answer. It was already too late at night to call the girl's house, but I called the airline and the airports in St. Louis and in Seattle. Alex was on a business trip at the time, so I was losing my mind that night alone. I never went to bed. Nathalie called me early next morning. There was no connection at the airport, she fell asleep in the car right after the girls' parents had picked her up, and was so tired she forgot to call me when she arrived at her friend's house. Kids!

At the same time, my preference for making our girls aware of their possible future choices in life instead of blind coercion to work did not mean that I was not pursuing academic excellence. The most imperative task at hand was for the girls to do well in school. Studying was the children's main responsibility, and they were expected to be responsible and do their best.

I continued to stimulate their intellectual and artistic curiosity, besides insisting they do their homework properly. As always, I was trying to educate them not only by direct words, but by creating a certain climate, a certain atmosphere conducive to an ever-growing desire for learning. I wanted them to see for themselves, and not only to hear it from Alex or me, that it paid to work hard. The first and critical step was to practice what we preached, but that came naturally. The girls have always seen how hardworking their father was, and I was never idle around the house either. It was also one more reason, besides the natural parental desire to give them the best, why I wanted our girls to have toys, clothes, exposure to travel, and other experiences commensurate and sometimes even slightly exceeding our family means. I did not want them to work to make up for what they were denied in childhood. I wanted them to want to work by exposing them to a way of life they would like to upkeep and explore more in depth when they grew up. While staying current with their supply of Barbie dolls and Nintendo games, not forgetting those cool overalls, I would consistently try to inculcate in them that a man does not live by bread alone. I would give them articles about current issues to read, with difficult words underlined and explained, to inspire them and help them see into themselves more clearly and determine their ethical values.

I would urge them to read books which I thought would enrich their lives. I would take them to major art exhibitions and theater performances. And we would travel domestically and internationally at every opportunity.

We were a young family with one source of income. I had to be enterprising. I believe the first application I filled in the United States in my own right was the application for a library card. For many years, getting the familiar white-and-black envelope in the mail, signifying the book I put a hold for was ready for pickup, would make my day. The first book I allowed myself to buy was *I Am Charlotte Simmons*, the 2004 novel by Tom Wolf. I was impatiently awaiting this book for what seemed an eternity. The girls were already in college, and I wanted an inside scoop on college life. Despite the book's chilling effect, I was satisfied by one thing. I did not need any more proof that good grades were not enough.

Helen Trepelkov

I knew by heart the free admission hours of all the major art museums and was much more familiar with the balconies of the major concert and theater venues than with their orchestras. The first time I bought a piece of clothing not on sale was when the girls were in middle school. In Gap. So I was sure there was room to grow.

As the girls became older, their specific interests and preferences became more visible. Nathalie could copy a painting at the Metropolitan Museum of Art even when she was as old as ten, but it would have been difficult to force her to go to a classical music concert, which Lydia consented to rather often. Lydia loved to join me for a modern ballet or a musical. Nathalie, on the other hand, would gobble up every book I suggested and then some, but Lydia preferred to choose her own reading. I accepted these differences and pushed the activities of my choosing less and less over the years. The engine was working. I did not have to jump-start or feed it anymore.

***

What seems so obvious now took some time to realize. When I came home from my first parent-teacher conference, I was so dumbfounded I could not understand where our girls stood. One of the precepts I was totally unfamiliar with was the "everybody is special in his or her own special way" one. The fact that junior school students were not always graded did not help either.

I liked the privacy of the encounter, however. In Russia, such conferences were, well, conferences. Everybody was gathered in one big hall, and by the end of it every parent knew everything about every student in the class. Needless to say, only a few got by unscathed, most had unkind feelings of various degree toward their offspring, depending on the degree of public humiliation they were forced to endure. Both parents and students mostly dreaded this embarrassing event.

In the Russian school of my time, one was graded practically the moment one stepped over the school threshold. I vaguely recall that we might have been given some slack in the first two or four months of the first grade, but I am not sure. No wonder. My first grades were certainly nothing to write home about, but I do very well remember the first time I brought home a notebook with big red "fives." I did not pay much attention to them at first. If anything, they just messed up my neat multicolored rows of squares, rounds, and vertical and slanted lines. But I saw how my mother's face lit up when she saw them, and I was happy to oblige, especially since colored pencils had been another passion of mine since I was three. I would draw, color, and sharpen them for hours. For many years my right-hand fingers had callouses caused by holding a pencil. Besides, if something made my mother happy, I reasoned, it was worth looking into.

Soon I was a straight-A, or rather straight-5, student. I graduated at the top of my class with a few other students who also had "all fives" through all my school and college years.

My mother, the first person who greeted me into this world, has always been a *sine qua non* of my existence. As my father liked to say, women are the keepers of the fire. She has always kept not only the fire of our house, our sanctuary, she has always kept the light burning bright inside of me.

Still, I was a matter-of-fact person and I wanted the truth. What did they mean by *special*? Was it some kind of a euphemism for *stupid*? I was convinced that children should learn to be responsible for their actions, and grades provided a measure to make sure everybody knew the exact worthiness of their effort. I never believed that such an approach could effectively prevent the onset of an inferiority complex or protect from any other negative effects, just postpone the awakening and make the adjustment so much more difficult since a lot of time might have been irrevocably lost. Shock came after shock. Unfamiliar ideas and concepts kept pouring in. I was astonished to hear a parent complain that her child was called fat by other kids and wanted the teachers to take action, and amazingly, the teachers acquiesced.

Don't get me wrong. It was not that I wanted overweight kids to be called fat and bad students to be called dumb. I am not especially bloodthirsty, but I felt these children were being dealt a very bad hand. I was sure parents could try and make their life nice for a few, maybe not so few years, but these kids would have to face reality sooner or later. And then what? They would have missed their opportunity to learn, and would have a very tough and painful awakening. I also felt that in a culture obsessed with good looks, maybe parents could pay more attention to their children's diet and make them both healthier and happier with themselves at the same time. I felt that not everyone was smart or beautiful, and people should not be penalized for it, but that does not mean people should allow themselves to let go and be lazy or gluttonous.

At about the same time I stumbled upon an article about the workforce requirements of the American economy. The American economy needs a relatively small percentage of super achievers. This explains the lack of objective, core incentives put on teachers to push students harder. The economy would still get its needed five or so percent naturally, because this is roughly the percentage of smart kids who tend to work well without external incentives. Still, the economy may not care whether it will employ student A or student B at a certain well-paid and interesting job, but it certainly could mean a world of a difference to those two students. I wanted our daughters to be at the top.

One evening, when I had already put the girls to bed, I started flipping through the pages of an old photo album. It was a huge leather-bound volume which contained all the girls' pictures from the moment they were born until they started school. I was slowly turning the pages, reliving each wonderful moment. Then I saw a picture of Lydia, in her pretty skating outfit I had so much fun knitting for her, on the day of her skating graduation party. All the memories came back in a flash. I realized I was back at the edge of that rink once again, figuratively speaking, my happiness theory put to the test.

Thinking over and analyzing my previous actions, I saw that at least partially the reason I felt so debonair about the kids' upbringing at that time could be the fact that we were part of the elite. Was I still contending that one should do what one loves or was I recanting and diverting to different ways? Now that we were not that privileged, that we had no safety net to fall back on, was I still pursuing my "happiness above all" idea? At that time, it looked like I was one step away from succumbing to the temptation and starting to earnestly devise our girls' destinies, while they were happily blowing their Bazooka bubbles. Would I, too, become like one of those parents at the rink, reining in their kids toward their bright future with an iron hand? Was I blinking? Should I blink? Did I have to sacrifice our children's happiness for them to succeed, or sacrifice success for them to be happy? Was there any way to tie the two together? I got my answers shortly thereafter.

When our girls' work begun to be graded, what struck me the most was the lack of strict preset requirements upon which the grades were based. Students had more or less specific requirements for the task, but their work was often graded on a curve, the best grade going to the best student. I was used to knowing in advance what I had to learn in order to get a certain grade. I had to read and memorize a certain material, or learn certain concepts, and I was judged according to my success in doing so, according to certain well-known, set-in-advance standards, independent of the results of other students. The fact that the best work was given the best grade, and the rest just followed suit, underscored a very important fact. The accent was not on the mastery of a certain body of knowledge, but on being the best. It is a much more competitive and unpredictable environment, which does not allow students to relax. One has to give all he or she has got. No one is pushing the child in school. This system calls for self-motivation, perpetual self-motivation, which makes doing your best the key component of success.

It meant that you could not achieve the best results by trying to force kids to study. It is just not practically feasible to push your children every time, everywhere and forever. As soon as they would have left the parental jurisdiction, be it to go to college or to start their first job, they could revert to their inner ways, whatever they would be at the time. Especially considering the ubiquitous practice not to stay in your parental house while getting a higher education degree and to leave for college often hundreds of miles away.

I realized that the only way for our daughters to be successful was to work hard of their own accord, of their own volition. Only then do we get a self-propelling device. No one can push you better than yourself, and you push yourself best and most rewardingly if you love what you do. Not only was my "happiness" idea acceptable, it seemed to be the most efficient one for the American system.

I did not want to force complicated degrees on our children, but I also did not want them to conscientiously choose jobs below their ability, to have a cozy, comfortable life. Personally, I don't believe there is such a thing as an easy life in less challenging fields anyway, and I did voice my opinion and tried to show what I meant at every suitable opportunity.

We did not encourage our daughters to work to earn money. We gave them reasonably good allowances and preferred them to use that time to study instead. Yet we did not say no when Lydia wanted to work as a waitress in our building's cafe during one of her high school summers. It turned out there was a lot of fighting for the coveted weekend evenings, which usually meant higher tips. I made sure I used this fact to get my point across as an example that there was no such thing as an easy life. You have to work hard and engage in some sort of politics no matter what you chose if you want to get to the top. There are no shortcuts.

In due time, the girls started the daunting college preparation process. Legacy, early admission, diversity, perfect fit—I was not familiar with any of these concepts. Moreover, despite all my epiphanies, I still had a very linear approach to success, in general, and scholastic success, in particular. The road to it was bright and straight with the gloriously shining image of Harvard at the end. I firmly believed that a Harvard degree was an indispensable external attribute of a truly successful life. I eventually broadened my list, after some hesitation, to include all of the Ivy League schools, but Harvard was still the paragon. I had no doubt in my mind that the girls had what it took, all they had to do was to work hard enough.

I wished I had an opportunity to try my own hand at getting accepted to Harvard. I was itching to take on this exciting challenge. I even was surreptitiously doing the girls' practice SAT tests while they were in school and started to work on their vocabulary flash cards that I bought while they were still in middle school. This little mania of mine certainly did not help to keep a level head.

The Stuyvesant School seemed like a good launching pad, but an advice from one of the fellow class mothers effectively prevented me from persevering in this direction. Sometime later, I found confirmation of her idea in an article on the subject. Colleges were interested in maintaining a certain level of diversity of their student body and could not accept but a certain amount of the best students from any particular school. The enormous amount of very smart kids at Stuyvesant and the inability to accept them all to the Ivy League institutions created a certain bottleneck that led to competition at a particularly high level and, on top of that, made unhealthy forms of it very tempting. It looked like it would be more reasonable to stay at UNIS, which usually had a good amount of admittances to the top universities.

The goal was to be one of the best students of the class. Only the top few had a chance. Your school's best could not be good enough for Harvard that particular year, or for any other Ivy League school, for that matter, but it was an absolute prerequisite for even considering one of such colleges. Of course, there were also such considerations as legacy. And then, of course, the notorious "oboe player". What if a trombone player was needed that particular year? What luck has got to do with it? It seemed preposterous, unfair to the utmost degree.

I never relied on pure dumb luck. I firmly believed in the infallibility of hard work. When I would come home after the exams in school or college, I would often tell my mother or grandmother that I was very lucky to draw the ticket with questions I knew perfectly well. Every time, they would laugh and say that one is always lucky when one is well prepared. I ended up believing it.

Gradually, I started to realize that the college acceptance process was to a great extent beyond the student's control. The workload would have to be huge and even so, there were no guaranties. Even being the best was ultimately not enough. I learned that each year, many kids with perfect grades and perfect SAT scores did not make the cut. Colleges were living organisms with a complicated set of requirements, with their specific goals, whims and quirks. One did not have to just have perfect grades, one had to perfectly fit in.

At about that time I got a warning signal. I had heard many stories about unsuccessful parental attempts to dragoon their kids into schools and courses of their own choosing, but this one somehow stuck out, maybe because the timing was so perfect. An old acquaintance of ours, an economist herself, was pushing her daughter, a college student, towards a degree in economics. The girl complied for some time, but finally rebelled when the workload in the dreaded subject became unbearable. She tried to switch to premed, only to realize that it was too late and she would not have time to fulfill all the requirements by her graduation. After a few last-minute vacillations she wound up with a random degree, at which point we lost touch with the family. From then on, I tried to hold my horses and keep my own dreams and vanities to myself. I did not succeed every time, and I did give bad advice on course selection on occasion, carried away by my own preferences and strengths, but remembering that story helped to keep me in check, most of the times.

The girls had a great college counselor, who held regular help clinics for parents and had a lot of advice tailored to each specific student. She was the one who introduced me to the "big fish in a small pond versus small fish in a big pond" concept. My maximalist self still rebelled against anything less ambitious than a big fish in a big pond. It seemed to be such a slippery slope. I was afraid that by following the desire to be a big fish in a small pond one could easily wind up in a pond small enough for just one fish. With time I had to agree that there was more than one way to skin a cat and that, come to think of it, used wisely, it was a great way to accrue one's worth in an environment with a manageable level of competition without running the risk of being destroyed by bigger fish right from the start. I realized that I have already chosen this path once when I stopped considering the Stuyvesant High school for the girls.

It was hard to wean myself from my obsession with Harvard. Certainly, much harder than to accept red sneakers worn with a turquoise skirt. The disconnect between my "happiness above all" concept and my firm belief in pure academic achievement that existed on different planes until that time, disappeared for good.

***

There was a rather popular idea, at least at that time, which was obviously in full accord with the idea of the priority of the child's natural proclivities, that students don't have to choose their future occupation from the very first college years, that they should take their time, get a liberal arts education, analyze their inclinations, mature, and then make a well-thought-out decision about their future career later.

I did not approve of this idea, however. I felt we could not afford this luxury. I feared that the girls, considering our family's lack of roots in this country, would not have time to acquire the knowledge and exposure to an extensive social network that would make such prolonged soul-searching beneficial. One should be very well familiar with the surroundings not to get lost while wandering about. This was when I remembered the James Bond joke, which was very popular among freshmen when I entered college myself in Moscow: James Bond is trying to get into our college. After a few futile attempts, he manages to get in. His authorities instruct him to just do everything exactly as all the other students do. He fails at the very first round of exams and is expelled. During debriefing, he swears he did everything as instructed. Other students cut classes, and he cut classes, other students copied homework, and he copied homework, but everybody passed the exams, and he failed.

The joke implied that many students had protection in high places and could afford to slack off. Our school was practically the only school in the country to graduate those who were going to get foreign assignments. No wonder there was a halo of elitism about the institution, and the student body had an abnormally large ratio of big shots' progeny. I guess many of us enjoyed this hype, it made us feel special, it tantalized the feelings of self-importance and flattered our for the most part still unworthy selves.

Anyway, back to the reason I mentioned the joke. It was just a joke, one of many we had, but its point was no laughing matter. The lesson of it was very salient, not to copy blindly and mindlessly what other people do, but to always look for the inner springs, being wary of superficial connections. I felt that it would be much more efficient for our girls to enter the highway of life right after college, that they needed to have a good solid skill, a métier by their graduation. That was my only concession to those parents at the rink.

After I realized that the best way to succeed in America was doing what one loves, the concept that "every child is special in her or his own special way" and the promotion of self-esteem appeared in a totally new light. It did not seem to be simply the desire of a nation to reap the benefits of the hard work of previous generations, as I previously thought. I saw the other side of it. Children are not stigmatized and pushed into some arbitrary direction from the very beginning. They are not given a matrix to conform to or a set of required achievements to meet. Children are free to remain themselves and still have a great shot at being successful, provided they work hard at becoming really good at what they love doing.

The American educational system provides a mechanism that, on one hand, makes sure that the economy gets the best person for the job, and on the other hand, allows the individual to succeed in what she or he loves doing. Like with the final turn of the Rubik's cube, everything clicked into place. I was on my yellow brick road.

Chapter Nineteen

We hear more and more that America is falling behind as far as its educational system is concerned. Is it really? I have a hard time accepting the notion that one of the most developed countries has one of the most outdated educational systems. It just does not make sense. Most likely, America hit the ceiling earlier than other nations, and started to search for alternatives.

Besides, could we just be using an outdated measuring stick? Are American students behind the students of many other developed countries in literacy or math skills? Absolutely! But maybe for everybody to follow in the press the progress of the imminent demise of humanity and accurately assess the probability for us to make it through another year is less important at this point than to forge a community able to solve our issues. Maybe now the accent is shifting away from conformity to a certain standard to being oneself. That does not mean you are allowed to be lazy, you are just not penalized for not being an Einstein. You are respected as a human being. Could those new trends also be the offshoots of a totally new approach to education, warranted by changing exigencies of the modern world and by the emergence of some new economic patterns?

The issues our world is facing are becoming more and more global in scope and call for our joint efforts. Economic globalization, the aggravation of the global problems stress the need to cooperate across many a difficult divide, pressure us to be more tolerant and more helpful to one another in order for us to survive as a species, for our planet to survive. As the latest developments demonstrate only too well, our very survival depends upon our wisdom and maturity. With the present levels of accumulation of weapons of mass destruction, we are well equipped to destroy ourselves from the outside. There is also a slew of purely ethical problems, created by the latest scientific developments, such as, for instance, experiments aimed at correcting mutations by manipulating the human genome, that if unaddressed could destroy humanity from within.

Such behavioral transformations would need an internal mechanism, a powerful objective driving forces closer to home. Whenever humanity faces a problem, however, there are usually solutions on the way. It appears these solutions could require a strict moral code not unlike the religious ones.

I remembered our high school chemistry teacher, who once told us that interdisciplinary problems usually call for philosophical interpretations and solutions.

The Golden Rule or ethic of reciprocity, encountered in many cultures and religions of the world, seems to be a principle woven with the rays of cosmic wisdom, beholding some higher truth, some absolute moral values indispensable to the survival of humanity as a species, in a way an encrypted survival road map.

Yet it also seems very far removed from reality, very much ahead of its time at best, and hardly attainable in the realistically near future. So far, life has never seemed to encourage brotherly love and kindness. It was more of a random phenomenon rather than a way of life, secular and religious appeals mostly disregarded. Would humanity ever be able to live by such principles? Ever look beyond its immediate self-interests? Could these values just be there waiting for the right moment, the moment when humanity would be mature enough to claim them, serving in the meantime as an ideal, resembling a faraway beacon, helping us not to get completely off course and showing us our final destination? After all, people are not often virtuous, true, but they know they have to be. Could the human society have just a blank spot ready for the future era of wisdom and moral integrity on its chart, like the table of chemical elements, which at first had a few blank spaces for yet undiscovered elements?

A single human being has three major strengths—physical, intellectual, and spiritual. Each one of these prevails at different stages of the individual life cycle. Youth satisfies primarily the needs of the body, mature age the needs of the mind, and old age is given the chance of being the age of wisdom. Human history could replicate this pattern and be a tortuous journey in the same direction, consecutively making the same three components a priority.

In the ancient societies, physical strength was a very valuable asset for the worker, vital for his survival. The labor-intensive forms of production prevailed, and medical science was not very prominent. These societies were not rich enough to sustain the sick and the old. One had to be strong to survive in the very unfriendly world. As a result of the scientific and technological progress, which brought about the Industrial Age, the emphasis shifted to intellectual capacities. The Enlightenment does not coincide with the Industrial Revolution by pure luck. It symbolizes the advent of the era of the intellect. Our times are the times of education and knowledge. The transition was made possible by the proliferation of machines making our work less strenuous, and as a result, the brain power became the key factor, superseding physical power. The third stage should then, logically, by sheer extrapolation, be the era of wisdom.

Moral integrity and high ethical norms should become the commodity of choice. For one thing, computerization and automation are already making huge encroachments and taking over certain intellectual activities. A 2013 Oxford study, for example, concludes that nearly half of all occupations in the United States are potentially automatable, perhaps within a decade or two. That would prepare the soil for a shift to a higher strength, but it still does not explain the need of the economy for high morality. What could bring about these changes?

More and more we hear of the need for a new workforce. We need creative people who can work as a team. The demand for creativity, teamwork, and cooperation in the work environment could probably make competition, the cornerstone of the present economic system, obsolete over time. In practical terms, it means the remuneration would have to be increasingly dependent not on the personal input, but on the common outcome, requiring forgoing certain self-interests, and as a result the supremacy of collaborative skills over the fighting ones.

As long as the main driving force of the society is competition, the advent of ethics as an economic principle does not seem possible.

Only when a high level of morality becomes economically beneficial would the change occur. It is not realistic to expect humans to think about the well-being of others when one is supposed to make a living by competing with them. Competition, surely, while bringing the best in us intellectually and physically, pitches us against one another, it separates us

Helen Trepelkov

instead of uniting. Can a group of exceedingly competitive and unforgiving kids play a board game? Sooner or later, the one who loses will be called names and the contenders will stop at nothing to win. Isn't that what happens, more or less, in the real world?

At the onset of the industrial age, competition provided a huge increase in productivity, allowing the choice of the best from a huge pool of labor. The nature of the work process is, however, changing. The worker does not produce his product from start to finish and even the belt conveyor taking care of an assembly line cannot do the trick anymore. Products nowadays, due to their increasing complexity, require an ever greater collaborative effort of a team of individuals to produce it. On the other hand, as many problems become increasingly complex and interconnected, it becomes imperative to further boost collaboration in order to find solutions that are beyond the scope of any single company or institution. The nature of these problems does not require mutually advantageous cooperation, but rather commonly advantageous cooperation, often foregoing less important self-interests in order to satisfy a common, more important one. The open source software or the social impact phenomena seem to point in that direction. All involved become one system, one organism, like the human body. As a result, whether the human nature undergoes actual changes or not, it would become increasingly profitable to act ethically.

The heart does not fight the lungs in our body, and the blood cells do not bring havoc to our blood supply by fighting for the top position, for the well-being of the heart depends upon the well-being of the lungs, of the whole body, and none of the blood cells has any advantage over the others from that perspective, either. The principle of treating others as one would like others to treat oneself does not seem so impossible at this point.

Maybe competition is on the verge of exhausting its potential. Each society, when engaging the individual in the work process, is destructive toward this individual in varying degrees. Competition compared for instance with slavery and serfdom, has been the least destructive so far, but it still leaves a great part of the individual's potential unused or even destroyed. Teamwork based on collaboration is a much more efficient form of labor organization. It makes use of a greater amount of human resources and causes less of their waste. So, as the next step, just maybe we will need everyone, every scrap of human resources we can get. The need to perpetually increase the productivity of labor would require it. We conserve energy, we worry about our footprint. We recycle soda cans. Maybe the time will come when we will treat with the greatest care the most valuable commodity—the human being. Nature abhors a vacuum, but also, nature abhors waste. So, theoretically, a perfect society, to follow in nature's footsteps, should operate so as to have no waste of human resources.

Collaborative work is like playing in an orchestra. Everyone is playing according to a certain common score. No one is expendable, because everybody has a specific part. Everyone becomes valuable, underscoring the uniqueness and pricelessness of human life.

Successful collaboration could lead to synergy. On a global scale, the effect could be comparable to a chain nuclear reaction, to an explosion of creativity and achievement. Could we be talking about a new Tower of Babel? We could, but in order to get closer to God, we have to start speaking the same language again, His language, and to humbly respect the laws of our universe, His laws. Is there anything more humble and more dignified than that? The alternative seems to be to crash and burn.

Those are probably the constructs of a far future, but life is getting very fast-paced nowadays. On a lighter note, new technology is absolutely disastrous as far as heirlooms go, I have to note. My Disney tape collection, imagined and perceived as an heirloom for many future generations, now comes with an old VCR attached. Silver spoons seem to still retain their appeal, however.

The acknowledgment of our differences calls for educational patterns to match. Maybe the trends that I witnessed when our children were studying in grade school were a sign that America was on its way toward a new, more efficient educational model for these are exactly the qualities that are increasingly required in the new work field. Maybe the stress on our diversity and self-esteem are the attempts to create a new human being— more secure, less thwarted by his limitations, and more attuned to his strengths and talents, the best that each of us can be. One would never be able to respect other people if one does not appreciate oneself. And respect for a human being should start from the cradle. The beginning of the new approach should not be grade school, not even kindergarten. The beginning is when the mother looks for the first time at her new child. In order for our democracies to be truly democratic, we should eliminate the age-old stronghold of tyranny from our households, the tyranny of parents over their children.

***

When our girls were graduating from middle school, they both had the same homework assignment—to write an autobiography. I did not give this assignment much thought at the time. To me it was just another project, but more original and fun.

I did not fully appreciate the usefulness of this endeavor until I started working on this book. Looking back at one's life automatically involves some amount of self-assessment. It helps to better understand who you are and consequently what you need to do to get where you want to be. This is especially beneficial to young people, who, having thus evaluated their lives and hopefully drawn some useful conclusions, still have their whole lives ahead of them to make some worthy corrections. For older folks, on the other hand, who have to sadly more or less draw a line under the toils of their lives, it could give some sort of closure. If they are lucky enough to deem their life a success, that is.

Actually, this is quite a scary thing, come to think of it. It is apparent, in hindsight, how useful it would have been to stop a few times along the road, look back and ask oneself the question, "How have I been doing so far?" Well, I did stop a couple of times along the way, but not nearly enough. The present was so overwhelming, so exciting, I had no time or desire to analyze the past, and was totally disinclined to succumb to any form of retrospection or introspection, for that matter. This is why, case in point, I did not appreciate the assignment in the first place. Well, it is one more reason to do so now.

I got swept off my feet by the possibilities and the challenges of motherhood. It took my breath away and forever changed my life.

The twenty years from the birth of our older daughter to my saying good-bye to our younger one on the steps of the Leavey Center of Georgetown University were the happiest years of my life.

Raising our children has not been a nuisance or a duty; certainly not an unavoidable byproduct of married life. It has not been a tepid affair, either, or a raging fire that consumes and disfigures everything it touches. It has been a steady and very intense glow that has made me a stronger and better person. I grew up and learned with our kids. Being able to raise our children was not a chore, it was not even work. It was a privilege and an honor.

Childbirth was to me akin to witnessing a huge, beautiful sunrise, full of potential, powerful, magnificent, yet enveloped in mystery. Holding a newborn was like holding a young universe, if just for a brief moment, being careful not to ruin or bruise it, before releasing it into our big world for everyone to behold and to enjoy. Everything paled in comparison as the stars and the moon disappear from the firmament when the sun rises. And since my very early childhood, I knew what being in the sun felt like. I would not have traded it for anything else.

Acknowledgments

I want to thank my parents for raising me strong enough and independent enough to do what I loved no matter how unpopular that may have been.

Thanks to my parents, I grew up free of old grudges and unsatisfied desires, used to a charmed life and determined to keep it that way. As a result, I fell in love with what seemed to me the most exciting and challenging career—motherhood. To run truly free one has to learn a lot and obey a lot of rules. Freedom is not blithe oblivion and reckless driving. Freedom is knowing where you are going and listening to your GPS, enjoying the scenery and the experience along the way. My parents did not tell me where to go. They gave me a very good GPS. And I have arrived.

I'm also grateful to my husband, who is now enjoying the beautiful city view not only from his apartment, but from his corner UN office as well, for accepting me the way I am, supporting me no matter how different our views might be.

My life was full of searching, doubts, and fears, but also of true joy, happiness, and victories. I tried to use every piece of knowledge, every scrap of information I learned to make our girls healthier, smarter, and happier. Looking back at those years, I perceive myself as a primordial gatherer, bringing home every experience, every bit of human achievement, so that our girls' childhood, when they looked back on it, would be shining and glittering, full of priceless treasures, like the Cave of Wonders.

I was once wandering around the historical center of Cartagena, Colombia. There was a statue of Simon Bolivar on a beautiful leafy square. I rarely read inscriptions on monuments, but the name of Bolivar has such a romantic ring to it, I approached this one. It read, "Cartagenians: if Caracas gave me life, Cartagena gave me glory." I was standing there for some time. I first heard about Simon Bolivar from my father. Who knows, maybe many years ago he stood in the exact same spot and was reading these words, too. I am very far from an historical figure. My personal failures and victories are far from being important enough to be put on the geographical map or be included in history books. But like every single person walking the earth in the quest for happiness, I had my Waterloos and I had my Cartagenas. And on my own personal scale, I can repeat after Bolivar, Russia gave me life and the United States gave me, if not glory, then certainly a sense of personal achievement.

I am very grateful to my daughters for turning out quite lovely and successful. The annoying thing about life is one doesn't always have time to leisurely ponder one's next move. More often than not, one has to think and act fast, shoot from the hip. As if that were not complicated enough, life rarely provides us with the luxury of second chances even when we realize we did something wrong. I am sure I made my share of mistakes. But it takes two to tango (three, actually, in this case), and I'm grateful to my daughters for wisely ignoring those mistakes and doing the right thing, which allows me to snag at least part of the credit by attributing their successes to my steady stewardship and claim victory.

Now I can sit back, relax, and just watch our children fly.

Thank you, my little ones, and Godspeed!

About the Author

Helen Trepelkov graduated *summa cum laude* with a master's degree in International Economic Relations from the Moscow State Institute for International Relations, dubbed the "Harvard of Russia" by Henry Kissinger. Shortly after, she followed her husband to New York City and unexpectedly became a stay-at-home mother.

Helen still lives in New York City with her husband and is now a stay-at-home grandmother, helping her two daughters, both graduates of Georgetown University, raise their children.

View other Black Rose Writing titles at www.blackrosewriting.com/books and
use promo code **PRINT** to receive a **20% discount** when purchasing.

BLACK🌹ROSE
writing™

91130619R00113

Made in the USA
Middletown, DE
28 September 2018